Land of the ANCESTORS

"Expropriation a Necessity for Justice"

JUSTICE SEUTLOALI

Copyright © 2024 Justice Seutloali

All rights reserved.

ISBN: 9798227675552

DEDICATION

This book is dedicated to my family, who have supported me throughout the long days and longer nights of writing. My son Shaka and my grandmother Ms Meipone Seutloali, and the rest of my family have all been a constant source of encouragement and inspiration. Their unwavering belief in me has made this journey possible.

CONTENTS

Acknowledgments
Acronyms and Abbreviations.
Preface

Introduction: Land, Power and History - The Unfinished Business of South Africa 1

1 Historical Background and the Brutality of White Settlers 9

Indigenous Wisdom and Colonial Disruption 13

Traditional Land Management Practices of the Zulu and Xhosa Peoples 16

Arrival of European Settlers and the Beginning of Land Dispossession 20

The Legacy of the Group Areas Act 25

Post-Apartheid Land Reform: Challenges and Progress 32

Conclusion 35

2 Land Expropriation without Compensation a Necessity for Justice 39

Challenges & Opportunities in Implementing Land Reform in S.A 44

The Slow Pace of Land Reform 48

Strategic Planning for Economic Stability in Land Expropriation 53

Learning from Global Land Reform Experiences 58

Conclusion 63

3 The Land is Rightfully Ours "Umhlaba Ngowethu" 67

Significance of the Nguni Peoples in South Africa's Land Struggles 69

The Khoisan: Guardians of the Land and Culture 74

	The Bantu Expansion and Its Impact on Southern Africa	77
	Conclusion	81

Table of Contents

4	**Through the Barrel of a Gun: Misconceptions and Propaganda**	84
	The "White Genocide" Narrative	86
	Misinterpretation of Land Reform Aspirations	90
	The Legal and Peaceful Process of Land Reform	94
	Conclusion	96
5	**Revising Section 25 to Effect Land Expropriation**	99
	The EFF's Motion for Expropriation Without Compensation	101
	Learning from International Land Expropriation Experiences	104
	Conclusion	107
6	**Voices from the Ground**	110
	Land as Identity and Ancestral Heritage	111
	The Role of Women and Youth in Land Reform	116
	The Urban Land Crisis in South Africa	123
	Conclusion	127
7	**The case for regime change**	129
	Regime Change and Radical Land Reform	131
	The Potential Impact of New Political Leadership	135

Conclusion 139

Table of Contents

8 The Economic Benefits of Land Expropriation — 141
Unlocking Economic Potential Through Equitable Land Distribution — 144

Land Access as a Catalyst for Rural Economic Growth — 147

The Interplay between Infrastructure and Economic Development — 150

Enhancing Investment Attraction through Secure Land Reform — 152

The Role of Land Reform in Promoting Social Equity — 155

Conclusion — 158

9 The Positive Impact of International Influence on Land Reform — 161
The World Bank's Impact on South Africa's Land Reform — 164

NGOs and International Organisations on South Africa's Land Reform — 168

Positive Impact of Foreign Investment on South Africa's Land Reform — 173

Impact of International Partnerships on Local Livelihoods — 176

Economic Development through International Collaboration — 180

Conclusion — 181

10 The Path Forward: Shaping the Future of Land Reform in S.A — 185
Addressing Persistent Challenges in Land Reform — 190

Unlocking Economic Potential Through Land Reform — 195

Conclusion — 201

Conclusion: Unity and Justice Through Land Expropriation — 203

Bibliography 210

About the Author 214

ACKNOWLEDGMENTS

The journey of writing *Land of the Ancestors: Expropriation a Necessity for Justice* has been both challenging and rewarding, and it would not have been possible without the support and contributions of many people and institutions.

I am deeply grateful to my mentors, colleagues, and friends whose insights, critiques, and expertise have greatly enriched this work. Your thoughtful feedback and constructive suggestions have been invaluable, and your dedication to justice and equity has been a constant source of inspiration.

A special thanks is due to the research institutions and libraries that provided access to crucial resources and references. Your dedication to preserving and sharing knowledge has been instrumental in shaping the depth and breadth of this book. Your commitment to academic excellence and intellectual rigour is greatly appreciated.

To the organisations and activists working tirelessly for land reform and social justice, your courage and commitment have been a source of inspiration and motivation. This book is dedicated to the collective struggle for a more equitable South Africa, and I hope it contributes to the ongoing efforts to achieve meaningful change.

Finally, I extend my gratitude to the readers and supporters of this book. Your interest and engagement with the issues of land expropriation and justice affirm the importance of this work and encourage ongoing dialogue and action. Your support and encouragement have been instrumental in bringing this project to fruition.

Thank you all for your contributions, your belief in the necessity of this important discussion, and your steadfast commitment to justice and equity.

ACRONYMS AND ABBREVATIONS

TRC – Truth and Reconciliation Commission
AFRICOM – United States Africa Command
FAO – Food and Agriculture Organisation
UNDP – United Nations Development Programme
NGO – Non-Governmental Organisation
GDP – Gross Domestic Product
EC – European Commission
UN – United Nations
SA – South Africa
NP – National Party
EFF – Economic Freedom Fighters
ANC – African National Congress
RDP – Reconstruction and Development Programme
PLA – People's Liberation Army
BEE – Black Economic Empowerment
REI – Rural Economic Initiatives
TAC – Treatment Action Campaign
CBO – Community-Based Organisation
GNP – Gross National Product
MKP – Umkhonto we Sizwe Party
SMMEs – Small, Medium, and Micro Enterprise
EWC - Expropriation without Compensation

PREFACE

South Africa's land is not merely a physical entity; it embodies a profound historical and cultural significance. *Land of the Ancestors: Expropriation a Necessity for Justice* explores the complex and often painful issues surrounding land ownership and restitution in South Africa.

The historical narrative of South Africa is deeply intertwined with its land. For centuries, indigenous communities have maintained a spiritual and cultural connection to their ancestral lands, which are integral to their identities and ways of life. This profound connection was disrupted by systemic dispossession and exploitation through colonisation and apartheid. The repercussions of these injustices continue to shape the nation's social and economic landscape, influencing current debates on land expropriation and restitution.

This book provides a thorough examination of how land expropriation without compensation—an issue that has garnered significant political and social attention in recent years—fits within the broader context of South Africa's historical and ongoing struggles. It traces the evolution of land reform policies from the early 20th century to the present day. The notion of expropriating land without compensation has generated considerable debate, reflecting deeper issues of equity, justice, and the enduring legacy of apartheid's land policies.

Land of the Ancestors aims to highlight the experiences and perspectives of those most affected by these policies. Through detailed case studies and personal narratives, the book captures the voices of indigenous communities advocating for the return of their ancestral lands. These stories of dispossession, resistance, and resilience are central to understanding the broader implications of land reform and underscore the human cost of historical injustices.

The book also addresses the legal and political dimensions of land expropriation without compensation. It examines the legislative frameworks and policy proposals that have emerged in response to demands for land reform. By exploring the successes and shortcomings of these policies, *Land of the Ancestors* offers a critical analysis of their effectiveness and the challenges that lie ahead.

In addition to historical and legal perspectives, this book considers the economic implications of land expropriation. The debate over compensation is not merely a financial issue but is intricately linked to broader questions of economic inequality and development. Understanding these economic dimensions is crucial for evaluating the potential outcomes of land reform policies and their impact on the nation's future.

Land of the Ancestors also explores the role of civil society and grassroots movements in shaping the land reform agenda. Activists, scholars, and community leaders have been instrumental in advocating for indigenous land rights and influencing policy decisions.

As South Africa continues to navigate the complexities of land reform, acknowledging and addressing the historical injustices that have shaped the current landscape is essential. This book aims to foster a deeper understanding of these issues and contribute to the ongoing dialogue about land restitution and reconciliation. It serves as both a historical account and a call to action, encouraging readers to consider the moral and practical implications of land reform.

By examining the past and its impact on the present, *Land of the Ancestors* hopes to inspire a more informed and empathetic approach to addressing land injustices. Confronting the complexities and contradictions inherent in the land reform debate is vital for working towards a future where all South Africans can benefit from a truly just and inclusive society.

Ultimately, land represents more than just a commodity; it is a fundamental aspect of cultural identity and heritage. The stories and struggles captured in these pages reflect a broader quest for recognition, justice, and dignity. As we move forward, understanding the legacy of land dispossession and the current debates surrounding land expropriation without compensation is crucial for achieving a future marked by justice and reconciliation.

May this book serve as a valuable resource for those seeking to understand the deep-seated issues of land reform and as a source of inspiration for those committed to advancing the cause of justice and reconciliation in South Africa.

Justice Seutloali
11 July 2022

INTRODUCTION: LAND, POWER AND HISTORY - THE UNFINISHED BUSINESS OF SOUTH AFRICA

Land expropriation has become central and contentious issue in contemporary South Africa, reflecting deep-seated historical injustices and ongoing socio-economic disparities. The discourse surrounding land reform, particularly the policy of land expropriation without compensation, is complex and multifaceted, touching on themes of justice, equity, and national identity. As Julius Malema, the leader of the Economic Freedom Fighters (EFF), passionately states, "We are not calling for the slaughtering of white people. At least for now. What we are calling for is for land expropriation without compensation to be implemented."[1] This provocative statement underscores the urgency and intensity of the land debate in South Africa today.

The history of land dispossession in South Africa is marked by systemic and pervasive injustices. During the colonial era, European powers, including the British and the Dutch, imposed their control over vast tracts of land, disregarding the existing land rights of indigenous African communities. This land was often acquired through coercive means, including treaties signed under duress, forced removals, and outright theft. The discovery of valuable resources, such as gold and diamonds in the late 19th century, intensified the land dispossession process. Colonial authorities and mining companies aggressively acquired land, displacing many African communities and consolidating land ownership in the hands of a few. This displacement was accompanied by discriminatory policies that aimed to marginalise and exploit the black population, further entrenching social and economic inequalities.[2]

---

[1] J Malema, 'We are not calling for the slaughter of white people, at least for now' (Speech, EFF Rally, 2016)
[2] Mahmood Mamdani, *Citizen and Subject: Contemporary Africa and the Legacy of Late*

The establishment of apartheid In 1948 formalised and codified racial segregation and land dispossession. The National Party government implemented a series of laws designed to entrench white supremacy and economic dominance, including the Group Areas Act, the Native Land Act, and the Bantustan policies. These laws restricted black South Africans' access to land and property, confining them to designated areas and severely limiting their economic opportunities. The Native Land Act of 1913 was particularly significant. It restricted black land ownership to just 7% of the country's land area and prohibited blacks from purchasing land outside these areas.[3] This act had a profound impact on black communities, leading to overcrowding, poverty, and the erosion of traditional land management practices. The Bantustan policy further exacerbated these issues by creating artificial tribal homelands that were economically unviable and isolated from major economic centres.[4]

***

With the end of apartheid in 1994, South Africa embarked on a process of political and economic transformation aimed at addressing the injustices of the past. Land reform became a key component of this transformation, with the goal of redressing historical imbalances and promoting equitable land distribution. The new democratic government, led by the African National Congress (ANC), adopted a land reform programme that included land restitution, land redistribution, and land tenure reform. The Land Restitution Act of 1994 provided a mechanism for Individuals and communities who had been dispossessed of land under apartheid to claim restitution. The Land Redistribution Act of 1994 aimed to provide land to previously disadvantaged individuals and communities to promote equitable land ownership.[5]

The Land Tenure reform Act sought to improve land rights for those living in communal areas, ensuring more secure tenure. Despite these

---

Colonialism (Princeton University Press 1996).
[3] The Native Land Act 1913 (SA) s 2.
[4] Deborah Posel, *The Making of Apartheid: 1948-1961* (Oxford University Press 1991)
[5] Land Restitution Act 1994 (SA).

efforts, the land reform programme has faced significant challenges. The pace of land reform has been slow, with many claims unresolved and land redistribution falling short of its targets. Moreover, the process has been marred by inefficiencies, corruption, and inadequate support for new landowners. As a result, the legacy of land dispossession continues to affect many South Africans, contributing to ongoing socio-economic disparities.

In recent years, the debate around land expropriation without compensation (EWC) has gained prominence. This debate is driven by the perceived inadequacies of the current land reform programme and the growing frustration among many South Africans about the slow pace of change. Proponents of EWC argue that it is a necessary step to accelerate land redistribution and address the deep-rooted injustices of the past. The idea of expropriating land without compensation is not new, but it has gained renewed attention in the context of the broader land reform debate. The notion of EWC was first introduced in the South African political discourse by the Economic Freedom Fighters (EFF), a political party led by Julius Malema. The EFF has argued that the current land reform mechanisms are insufficient and that EWC is needed to rectify historical wrongs and promote economic justice.[6]

In 2018, the South African Parliament began a process to explore the feasibility of amending the Constitution to allow for land expropriation without compensation. This move was prompted by the EFF's proposal and growing support from various sectors of society. The proposed amendment sought to enable the state to expropriate land without compensation for the purposes of land redistribution, with the aim of addressing the legacy of dispossession and promoting economic transformation.[7] The proposal for constitutional amendment has sparked a heated debate. Supporters argue that EWC is essential for correcting historical injustices and addressing the economic disparities that continue to affect black South Africans. They contend that compensation often benefits those who acquired land through unjust

---

[6] Economic Freedom Fighters, *Land Reform Policy Document* (EFF, 2013).
[7] Parliament of South Africa, 'Constitutional Review Committee: Report on Land Expropriation' (2018).

means and that EWC is a way to return land to its rightful owners and promote economic empowerment.[8]

***

The socio-economic implications of land expropriation without compensation are significant and multifaceted. On the one hand, proponents of EWC argue that it could promote greater economic equity and social justice by redistributing land to previously disadvantaged communities. This, in turn, could lead to improved livelihoods, economic opportunities, and social cohesion. Access to land is crucial for economic development, particularly in rural areas where agriculture is a primary livelihood. By enabling land redistribution, EWC could provide disadvantaged communities with the means to engage in productive economic activities, improve food security, and enhance their overall quality of life. Additionally, addressing historical land injustices could help heal societal divisions and foster a sense of national unity.[9]

Furthermore, the implementation of EWC must be carefully managed to avoid exacerbating existing inequalities or creating new forms of injustice. Effective and transparent mechanisms are needed to ensure that land redistribution is fair and equitable, and that support is provided to new landowners to help them succeed. Failure to address these issues could undermine the potential benefits of EWC and lead to further socio-economic challenges.

The land debate in South Africa is also deeply intertwined with questions of identity, cultural heritage, and historical memory. Land is not merely a physical asset; it is a symbol of cultural identity, historical connection, and community cohesion. For many South Africans, land represents a vital link to their ancestral heritage and traditional practices. The legacy of land dispossession has had a profound impact on cultural identity and community life. The loss of land has disrupted traditional ways of life, eroded cultural practices, and contributed to a sense of

---

[8] Parliament of South Africa, 'Constitutional Review Committee: Report on Land Expropriation' (2018).
[9] Ben Cousins, *Land Reform in South Africa: An Overview* (PLAAS 2020)

disconnection from ancestral roots.[10]

Restoring land to its rightful owners is seen by many as a way to reclaim cultural heritage and reinforce cultural identity. At the same time, the process of land expropriation and redistribution must be sensitive to cultural considerations and respect the diverse needs of different communities. Ensuring that land reform efforts are inclusive and culturally appropriate is essential for achieving lasting and meaningful change. This requires engaging with communities, understanding their cultural values and practices, and developing land reform policies that reflect these considerations.[11]

Ultimately, the goal of land reform should be to promote justice, equity, and reconciliation while supporting economic development and social cohesion. Achieving this balance will require a nuanced understanding of the historical context, careful consideration of the socio-economic implications, and a commitment to inclusive and transparent processes. By addressing these challenges, South Africa can work towards a more equitable and just land tenure system that reflects its diverse and complex history.

***

Land of the Ancestors: Expropriation a Necessity for Justice embarks on an extensive exploration of the intricate issues surrounding land expropriation in South Africa, delving into its historical roots, legal frameworks, and socio-economic implications. The aim of this book is to offer a comprehensive analysis of the ongoing debate about land expropriation, highlight the historical injustices that have led to current policies, and evaluate the potential impacts these policies may have on the country's future. The central focus of the book is to understand the multifaceted drivers behind the demand for land expropriation without compensation.

This examination includes a deep dive into the historical context that

---

[10] Megan Vaughan, *Curing Their Ills: Colonial Power and African Illness* (Stanford University Press 1991)
[11] Ibid.

has shaped current attitudes and policies regarding land. The legacy of colonialism and apartheid has left a profound impact on land ownership and distribution in South Africa. Historical dispossessions, racial segregation, and discriminatory land policies have created long-standing inequalities that continue to resonate in contemporary land reform discussions. By tracing these historical injustices, the book aims to provide a thorough understanding of why the issue of land expropriation remains a critical and urgent concern.

The book seeks to address several fundamental questions central to the debate on land expropriation. One major question is how land expropriation policies align with broader goals of justice and equity. This involves assessing the ethical and moral implications of these policies and their potential to address historical wrongs. Land expropriation without compensation is often proposed as a solution to rectify past injustices and redistribute land more equitably.

The book evaluates whether these policies are likely to meet their intended goals and how they fit within the broader framework of social justice and equity. Another crucial aspect explored in the book is the potential social, economic, and political impacts of implementing land expropriation without compensation. The social repercussions of such policies are significant, potentially affecting community dynamics, social cohesion, and the relationships between different groups within society. Economic consequences are also substantial, as land expropriation can influence investment patterns, agricultural productivity, and overall economic stability.

Additionally, the political implications of these policies are examined, including potential shifts in power dynamics, governance structures, and the broader political landscape. To provide a comprehensive analysis, the book is organised into a series of chapters that address various facets of the land reform process. The initial chapters lay the groundwork by introducing the context and objectives of the book, outlining the scope of the study, and providing an overview of the key themes and questions being addressed. These chapters set the stage for a more detailed examination of the historical background of land ownership in South Africa.

Subsequent chapters delve into the historical context of land dispossession and the impact of colonial and apartheid policies on land ownership. The book explores how these historical factors have contributed to the current land reform challenges and the demand for expropriation without compensation. It provides a detailed account of the evolution of land ownership and use, highlighting how past injustices have shaped contemporary land policies.

The book also traces the evolution of land reform policies in South Africa. It examines the various phases of land reform, from early attempts at addressing land inequalities to the current focus on expropriation without compensation. This analysis includes a critical assessment of the successes and failures of past policies and their influence on the present debate. By understanding the progression of land reform efforts, the book aims to offer insights into the effectiveness of different approaches and their implications for future policies. A significant portion of the book is dedicated to analysing the implications of land expropriation without compensation.

This includes a critical examination of how these policies are implemented and their practical effects on landowners, communities, and society as a whole. In addition to the socio-economic and political impacts, the book explores legal perspectives on land expropriation. This involves examining the legal frameworks and regulations governing land reform and expropriation in South Africa. The legal analysis helps to understand the challenges and opportunities presented by current policies and how they align with constitutional and international standards.

The roles played by various political and civil society actors In the land reform process are also examined. The book looks at the positions and contributions of different stakeholders, including government agencies, political parties, advocacy groups, and affected communities. By considering the perspectives and actions of these actors, the book provides a more comprehensive view of the land reform landscape and the dynamics influencing policy development and implementation.

Land of the Ancestors: Expropriation a Necessity for Justice aims to contribute meaningfully to the ongoing dialogue on land reform and justice in South Africa. It is designed for scholars, policymakers, activists, and anyone interested in understanding the complexities of land expropriation and its role in addressing historical injustices. By providing a detailed analysis of the historical, legal, and socio-economic dimensions of land expropriation, the book seeks to foster a deeper understanding of the issues at stake and offer insights into potential paths forward for achieving justice and equity in land reform.

1. HISTORICAL BACKGROUND AND THE BRUTALITY OF WHITE PEOPLE

"The fight for land extends beyond merely acquiring property; it is a battle for the future of our people."[12] This insight profoundly captures the essence of the historical and ongoing conflict over land in South Africa. The land, in pre-colonial times, was not merely a resource for survival but an integral element of cultural identity, spiritual belief, and communal life. Before the arrival of European settlers, South Africa's land was managed and utilised by various indigenous communities through systems that were as sophisticated as they were diverse, reflecting a deep understanding of their environment and a complex relationship with it.[13]

Indigenous peoples such as the Khoikhoi, San, Zulu, and Xhosa had established intricate systems of land use and stewardship, each tailored to their specific ecological and social contexts.[14] These systems were grounded in a profound connection to the land, demonstrating that indigenous knowledge and practices were far from primitive; instead, they were advanced, adaptive, and remarkably sustainable.[15]

The Khoikhoi, for example, were primarily pastoralists who managed their herds of cattle with an exceptional grasp of their environment. Their understanding of land management was deeply rooted in their cultural practices and spiritual beliefs. The Khoikhoi's approach to managing their herds included rotational grazing, a practice that involved moving cattle between different pastures to prevent overgrazing and ensure that vegetation had time to recover.

This method was not just a practical solution to the problem of

---

[12] J Seutloali, *Speech at The EFF's Regional General Assembly* (2017) [De Aar].
[13] M N Mphahlele, The Indigenous Peoples of South Africa (University of South Africa Press 2011).
[14] Ibid.
[15] Ibid.

overgrazing but also a reflection of the Khoikhoi's respect for the land, which they viewed not merely as a resource but as a living entity deserving of care and attention. Their rotational grazing practices were informed by traditional ecological knowledge that had been passed down through generations. This knowledge encompassed an understanding of the land's carrying capacity and the need to maintain ecological balance.[16]

The Khoikhoi recognised that the land was a dynamic system, and their practices were designed to work within its natural cycles. By allowing pastures to rest and regenerate, they ensured that their agricultural activities did not lead to long-term environmental degradation.[17]

The San people, who were primarily hunter-gatherers, exhibited an equally sophisticated understanding of their environment. Their knowledge of the land was integral to their survival and way of life. The San's nomadic lifestyle meant that they moved through the landscape in a way that allowed natural processes to continue unhindered. Their intimate knowledge of plant and animal behaviour enabled them to exploit resources sustainably, ensuring that their impact on the environment was minimal.[18]

The Zulu and Xhosa communities, on the other hand, practiced a mix of agriculture and pastoralism, with each group developing unique methods suited to their specific environments. The Zulu, for instance, were known for their sophisticated agricultural techniques, which included the cultivation of staple crops such as maize and millet. Their farming practices were complemented by their knowledge of local soils and climatic conditions, allowing them to optimise their agricultural outputs while preserving soil fertility.[19]

The Xhosa people also had their own distinct land management practices, which included rotational farming and the careful selection of crop varieties suited to different soil types. Their agricultural practices were closely tied to their cultural and spiritual beliefs, with rituals and

---

[16] M N Mphahlele, *The Indigenous Peoples of South Africa* (n14)
[17] Ibid.
[18] Ibid.
[19] Jeffrey B Peires, *The House of Phalo: A History of the Xhosa People in the Days of Their Independence* (Ravan Press 1981).

ceremonies often marking important phases in the agricultural calendar. This integration of cultural practices with agricultural activities ensured that their farming methods were sustainable and deeply rooted in their social and spiritual values.[20]

The arrival of European settlers marked a dramatic shift in the management and utilisation of land in South Africa. The Europeans brought with them not only new technologies and agricultural practices but also a fundamentally different worldview. They viewed land primarily as a commodity, to be owned, controlled, and exploited for economic gain. This perspective was in stark contrast to the indigenous understanding of land as a communal resource, integral to the social and spiritual fabric of their communities.[21]

The imposition of European land ownership concepts led to the displacement of indigenous peoples and the disruption of their traditional land management systems. The settlers' pursuit of land for agriculture and mining resulted in the systematic dispossession of indigenous lands, which were often forcibly taken or expropriated under various pretexts. This process was accompanied by a range of violent and coercive tactics, including military confrontations, treaties that were often made under duress, and legal mechanisms designed to legitimise the appropriation of land.[22]

One of the most notorious examples of this violence was the series of conflicts known as the Frontier Wars, which were fought between the British colonists and the Xhosa people. These wars were characterised by brutal military engagements and widespread destruction of Xhosa property and settlements. The British sought to expand their territories and secure control over fertile lands, leading to numerous clashes with the Xhosa, who were defending their ancestral lands and way of life. The consequences of these wars were devastating, with large-scale displacement and loss of life among the Xhosa people.[23]

---

[20] Peires, *The House of Phalo: A History of the Xhosa People in the Days of Their Independence* (n19)
[21] Roger B. Beck, *The History of South Africa* (Oxford University Press, 2011).
[22] Ibid.
[23] N Mostert, Frontiers: *The Epic of South Africa's Creation and the Tragedy of the Xhosa People* (Jonathan Cape 1992)

The impact of European colonisation on the Khoikhoi and San peoples was equally severe. The introduction of European diseases, against which the indigenous populations had little immunity, led to a dramatic decline in their numbers. The Europeans also encroached upon Khoikhoi lands, disrupting their pastoralist practices and forcing them into new forms of economic dependency. The San, meanwhile, faced increasing pressure from settlers who encroached upon their traditional hunting grounds, leading to a loss of their traditional way of life and further marginalisation.[24]

The imposition of European land ownership concepts was formalised through a series of legal and administrative measures that entrenched colonial control over land. The introduction of land surveys, title deeds, and property laws created a framework that disregarded indigenous land tenure systems and effectively erased traditional land rights.[25] The British colonial administration, followed by the Union of South Africa and the apartheid regime, continued to enforce and expand these legal mechanisms, leading to the systematic dispossession of indigenous peoples and the consolidation of land in the hands of a few.[26]

Under apartheid, the dispossession of land and the enforcement of racial segregation were taken to new extremes. The government implemented a series of policies designed to segregate and control the movement of black South Africans, including the notorious Group Areas Act, which restricted black people to specific areas and further deprived them of their land.[27] The Bantu Authorities Act and the creation of homelands or Bantustans were part of a broader strategy to undermine the political and economic rights of black South Africans, consolidating control over land and resources for the benefit of the white minority.[28]

The legacy of colonial and apartheid land policies continues to shape the socio-economic landscape of South Africa today. The vast disparities

---

[24] R Elphick, *Khoikhoi and the Founding of White South Africa* (Ravan Press 1985).
[25] M Legassick, *The Struggle for the Eastern Cape 1800–1854* (Kegan Paul International 2010).
[26] P Maylam, *A History of the African People of South Africa: From the Early Iron Age to the 1970s* (David Philip Publishers 1986)
[27] L Thompson, *A History of South Africa* (Yale University Press 2001).
[28] C Walker, *Landmarked: Land Claims and Land Restitution in South Africa* (Jacana Media 2008)

in land ownership and access to resources are a direct result of centuries of dispossession and discrimination. The post-apartheid government has made efforts to address these injustices through land reform programmes aimed at redistributing land and providing restitution to dispossessed communities. However, progress has been uneven, and the challenge of achieving meaningful land reform remains a pressing issue.[29]

Indigenous Wisdom and Colonial Disruption

The historical background of land management in South Africa reveals a complex interplay of indigenous knowledge, colonial exploitation, and post-apartheid reforms. The indigenous peoples of South Africa demonstrated advanced and sustainable methods of land use that were deeply integrated with their cultural values and environmental understanding. The arrival of European settlers marked a dramatic shift in land management practices, characterised by dispossession, violence, and the imposition of new legal frameworks that disregarded indigenous systems. The legacy of these historical injustices continues to impact land ownership and access to resources in contemporary South Africa, highlighting the need for continued efforts to address the deep-seated inequalities that persist today.[30]

Their pastoral system was intricately linked to their social structures. For instance, Khoikhoi communities often employed a system of communal land tenure, where land was held collectively and managed through customary laws. The Khoikhoi's approach to land management was highly adaptable, with strategies that varied depending on seasonal conditions and the specific needs of their herds. Their practices not only ensured sustainable use of resources but also reinforced social cohesion and collective responsibility.

In contrast, the San people, who inhabited the arid and semi-arid regions of South Africa, led a hunter-gatherer lifestyle that was intricately

---

[29] Thompson, *A History of South Africa* (n27).
[30] Tembeka Ngcukaitobi, *The Land Is Ours: South Africa's First Black Lawyers and the Birth of Constitutionalism* (Penguin 2018)

tied to their profound understanding of seasonal changes and resource availability. Their subsistence strategies were a direct response to the challenging environment they lived in, which required an acute awareness of the land's rhythms to ensure survival.[31]

The San's way of life was characterised by their mobility, which was essential for accessing seasonal resources. They followed migratory patterns that were dictated by the movement of game and the growth cycles of edible plants. This nomadic lifestyle was not random but strategically planned to avoid overexploitation of any single area. By constantly moving, they allowed natural resources to regenerate and maintained a delicate ecological balance within their environment. This method of living was fundamentally sustainable, as it prevented the depletion of resources and ensured the continued availability of food and materials necessary for their survival.[32]

The San people possessed an extensive and detailed knowledge of animal behaviour and plant life, honed through generations of observation and experience. They understood the habits and patterns of various animals, which enabled them to track and hunt effectively. Their hunting techniques were sophisticated and adapted to the behaviour of different species, reflecting their deep engagement with the natural world.[33] The San were also skilled in identifying and utilising a wide range of edible plants, which provided a crucial supplement to their diet.[34]

Their understanding of the environment was not solely practical but also deeply embedded in their cultural and spiritual beliefs. Knowledge about resources, environmental changes, and survival strategies was transmitted through oral traditions, storytelling, and ceremonial practices. These methods of communication were vital for preserving and passing down crucial information. Elders played a key role in educating younger generations, ensuring that their extensive knowledge about the land, its resources, and the seasonal variations was retained and

---

[31] E Wilmsen, *Land Filled with Flies: A Political Economy of the Kalahari* (University of Chicago Press 1989)
[32] Ibid.
[33] M Biesele, *Women Like Meat: The Folklore and Foraging Ideology of the Kalahari Ju/'hoan* (Indiana University Press 1993)
[34] E Thomas, *The Harmless People* (Vintage Books 1989)

adapted as needed.[35]

The San's connection to the land was also expressed through their remarkable rock art, which serves as both a record and a communication tool. The rock art, found in various locations throughout South Africa, provides insights into their interactions with the natural world. These artworks often depict animals, hunting scenes, and ceremonial events, reflecting the San's relationship with their environment and their spiritual beliefs. The art was not merely decorative but carried significant cultural and symbolic meanings, documenting their experiences and conveying messages about their world.[36]

Through their rock art, the San communicated their understanding of the land's spiritual dimensions. The paintings and engravings often featured intricate depictions of animals and figures involved in ritualistic practices. These artworks were believed to be more than just representations; they were thought to hold spiritual significance and to be a means of connecting with the spiritual world. The San's artistic expressions offered a window into their worldview, illustrating how their environmental knowledge was interwoven with their cultural and religious beliefs.[37]

The San's lifestyle exemplified a harmonious relationship with their environment, achieved through an extensive body of knowledge, practical skills, and cultural practices. Their ability to live sustainably in a challenging environment was a testament to their deep understanding of the natural world and their capacity to adapt to its changes. The San's way of life, with its focus on mobility, resource management, and spiritual connection, demonstrated a profound respect for the land and its rhythms.[38]

Despite their remarkable adaptability and sustainability, the San faced significant challenges with the arrival of European settlers. The colonisation process disrupted their traditional way of life, leading to

---

[35] S R Schapera, *The Khoisan Peoples of South Africa: Bushmen and Hottentots* (Routledge & Kegan Paul 1930).
[36] E Wilmsen, *Land Filled with Flies: A Political Economy of the Kalahari* (University of Chicago Press 1989)
[37] Schapera, The Khoisan Peoples of South Africa: Bushmen and Hottentots (n35)
[38] Ibid.

displacement and marginalisation. The encroachment of settlers on their lands, coupled with the imposition of new economic and social systems, undermined their ability to maintain their nomadic lifestyle and traditional practices.[39]

The displacement and disruption of the San's way of life had far-reaching consequences. The loss of access to their traditional hunting grounds and the breakdown of their social structures contributed to their marginalisation and economic hardship. The introduction of new legal and economic systems further eroded their traditional land rights and ways of living. The San were often forced into new roles within the colonial economy, which were frequently exploitative and detrimental to their well-being.[40]

Despite these challenges, the San have continued to preserve and celebrate their cultural heritage. Efforts to document and revitalise their traditional knowledge and practices have been ongoing, reflecting a resilience and commitment to preserving their identity and history. The San's rich cultural and spiritual connection to the land remains an essential aspect of their identity, even as they navigate the complexities of the modern world.[41]

Traditional Land Management Practices of the Zulu and Xhosa Peoples

The Zulu and Xhosa peoples, who inhabited the diverse regions of South Africa, developed sophisticated systems of land management tailored to their unique environments and socio-cultural contexts. Their approach to land use was characterised by a combination of agriculture and pastoralism, reflecting a deep understanding of their surroundings and an emphasis on communal responsibility.[42]

---

[39] Richard B Lee, *The !Kung San: A Study in Human Ecology* (Cambridge University Press 1979).
[40] Ibid.
[41] Ibid.
[42] P Maylam, *A History of the African People of South Africa: From the Early Iron Age to the 1970s* (David Philip Publishers 1986)

For the Zulu, who primarily occupied the fertile regions of KwaZulu-Natal, land management was deeply intertwined with their social structure and cultural practices. Traditional Zulu society was organised around a system of communal land ownership . Land was held collectively by the community, and its allocation and use were overseen by a chief and his council of elders. This communal approach ensured that land was managed in a way that benefited the entire community rather than individual interests. The chief played a pivotal role in overseeing land distribution, making decisions about its use, and resolving disputes related to land. This centralised authority was crucial in maintaining order and ensuring that resources were allocated fairly.[43]

The Zulu system of land management was complemented by a rich tradition of rituals and ceremonies that marked agricultural cycles and reinforced social bonds. Agricultural activities were closely aligned with seasonal changes and spiritual beliefs. For instance, the Zulu held ceremonies to mark the planting and harvesting of crops, which were believed to ensure fertility and bountiful harvests. These rituals were not only significant for their practical impact on agriculture but also for their role in strengthening community cohesion and cultural identity. The ceremonies served as a means of reaffirming communal ties and expressing gratitude to the ancestors for their protection and guidance.[44]

The Zulu people practised a form of mixed farming that included both crop cultivation and livestock rearing. They grew staple crops such as maize, millet, and beans, which were supplemented by the rearing of cattle. The cattle played a central role in Zulu society, serving not only as a source of food but also as a form of wealth and social status. The management of cattle was closely regulated, with practices designed to ensure their health and productivity. This included rotational grazing to prevent overgrazing and allow pastures to recover.[45]

Similarly, the Xhosa people, who lived in the Eastern Cape region, also engaged in a combination of agriculture and pastoralism, but their

---

[43] P Maylam, *A History of the African People of South Africa: From the Early Iron Age to the 1970s* (David Philip Publishers 1986)
[44] Ibid.
[45] N Worden, *The Making of Modern South Africa: Conquest, Apartheid, Democracy* (Wiley-Blackwell 2012).

systems of land management were adapted to their specific environmental and social contexts. Like the Zulu, the Xhosa practiced communal land ownership, with decisions about land use being made collectively by the community. This system of land tenure reinforced social ties and fostered a sense of mutual responsibility and cooperation among community members.[46]

In Xhosa society, land was allocated based on family needs and agricultural requirements, with each family receiving a portion of land for cultivation. The communal approach to land management ensured that resources were shared equitably and that everyone had access to the land needed for farming and grazing. This system of collective decision-making helped to prevent conflicts and promote harmony within the community.[47]

The Xhosa also employed advanced agricultural techniques to maintain soil fertility and enhance productivity. Crop rotation and fallowing were key components of their farming practices. By rotating crops and allowing fields to rest, the Xhosa were able to prevent soil depletion and ensure that their land remained productive over the long term. These practices were supported by traditional knowledge and were integral to maintaining the health of the land.[48]

In addition to their agricultural practices, the Xhosa engaged in various forms of pastoralism, including the rearing of cattle, sheep, and goats. Livestock played a central role in Xhosa society, providing essential resources such as food, clothing, and trade goods. The management of livestock involved practices designed to ensure their well-being and productivity, including careful monitoring of grazing patterns and the provision of supplementary feeding during periods of drought.[49]

Both the Zulu and Xhosa systems of land management were deeply rooted in their cultural and social values. The communal approach to land ownership and decision-making reflected a broader ethos of

---

[46] Worden, *The Making of Modern South Africa* (n45)
[47] Jeffrey B Peires, *The House of Phalo: A History of the Xhosa People in the Days of Their Independence* (Ravan Press 1981)
[48] Ibid.
[49] Ibid.

collective responsibility and mutual support. By integrating agricultural practices with traditional rituals and social structures, these societies were able to maintain a sustainable and harmonious relationship with their environment.[50]

The arrival of European settlers marked a significant disruption to these traditional systems of land management. The imposition of colonial land policies, which prioritised individual land ownership and disregarded communal tenure systems, led to the displacement and marginalisation of the Zulu and Xhosa peoples. The introduction of new legal frameworks and economic systems further undermined their traditional practices and contributed to widespread social and economic upheaval.[51]

Sacred sites, burial grounds, and ritual spaces were integral to land management practices across these communities. Land was not merely viewed as a resource but as a repository of cultural and spiritual significance. Certain areas were designated for rituals and ceremonies, which reinforced the connection between the people and their land.

These sacred practices highlighted the belief that the land was imbued with ancestral spirits and that its management was a matter of spiritual and communal responsibility. For instance, the Zulu and Xhosa communities maintained sacred groves and ritualistic landscapes that were central to their cultural practices.

These sites were often associated with ancestor worship and the performance of rites that were believed to ensure the fertility of the land and the well-being of the community. The preservation of these sites was a key aspect of land management, reflecting the interconnection between cultural identity and environmental stewardship.

---

[50] Peires, *The House of Phalo: A History of the Xhosa People in the Days of Their Independence* (n47)
[51] R. Elphick and H Giliomee (eds), *The Shaping of South African Society, 1652-1840* (2nd edn, Wesleyan University Press 1989)

The Arrival of European Settlers and the Beginning of Land Dispossession

The arrival of European settlers In the 17th century heralded the beginning of a protracted and often violent era of land dispossession for South Africa's indigenous peoples. This period was marked by significant upheaval, as the expansion of European settlements led to profound changes in land ownership and use, often at the expense of the indigenous populations.[52]

In 1652, the Dutch East India Company established a supply station at the Cape of Good Hope, a strategic location for resupplying ships en route to the East Indies. Initially conceived as a logistical base, the settlement at the Cape rapidly expanded beyond its original scope. The early Dutch settlers, primarily Dutch farmers and traders, began to establish farms and build infrastructure, which inevitably led to encroachments on the surrounding lands inhabited by indigenous communities.[53]

The initial interactions between the Dutch settlers and the indigenous Khoikhoi people, who lived in the Cape region, were characterised by a complex mix of cooperation and conflict. The Khoikhoi, who had a system of pastoralism and land use that involved seasonal migrations and communal ownership, found themselves increasingly squeezed by the expanding European settlement. The settlers' growing demand for land and resources created tensions over land use, which were often exacerbated by misunderstandings and cultural differences.[54]

The Dutch East India Company's expansionist policies played a central role in these conflicts. As the settlement grew, Dutch authorities sought to increase their agricultural output and expand their territorial control. This expansion frequently came at the cost of indigenous land,

---

[52] R J. Gordon, 'European Settlements and Indigenous Dispossession in South Africa: A Historical Perspective' (2019)
[53] R. Viljoen, 'Aboriginal Khoikhoi Servants and Their Masters in Colonial Swellendam, South Africa, 1745-1795
[54] R. Elphick and H Giliomee (eds), *The Shaping of South African Society, 1652-1840* (2nd edn, Wesleyan University Press 1989)

which was often taken through coercion, violence, and the imposition of unequal treaties. These treaties, which were purported to be agreements, were frequently negotiated under duress or with significant power imbalances, leading to agreements that heavily favoured the settlers and undermined the land rights of the indigenous peoples.[55]

As the Dutch expanded their territory, they encountered resistance from various indigenous groups, including the Khoikhoi, who attempted to defend their land and way of life. The Dutch responded to these resistances with military force, leading to a series of violent confrontations known as the Khoikhoi-Dutch Wars. These wars, which spanned several decades, were marked by brutal tactics on both sides. The Dutch sought to subdue the Khoikhoi and assert control over the land, while the Khoikhoi fought to protect their territories and maintain their traditional way of life.[56]

The Impact of these conflicts was devastating for the indigenous communities. The combination of violent confrontations, disease introduced by Europeans, and the relentless pressure to cede land led to significant population declines and social disruption among the Khoikhoi. The Dutch settlement's expansion also led to the marginalisation and displacement of other indigenous groups in the region, further compounding the pressures faced by the local populations.[57]

The arrival of the Dutch settlers at the Cape marked the beginning of a broader pattern of European colonial expansion that would have profound implications for the indigenous peoples of South Africa. The Dutch East India Company's establishment of a permanent settlement at the Cape was only the start of a longer process of colonisation that would involve other European powers, including the British, who arrived in the early 19th century. Each wave of European expansion brought with it new policies and practices that further entrenched colonial control over land and resources.[58]

---

[55] R. B. Beck, *The History of South Africa* (Oxford University Press, 2011)
[56] Ibid.
[57] Ibid.
[58] Ibid.

The British arrival in the early 19th century introduced new dimensions to the land dispossession process. The British authoriti continued the practices of land appropriation and displacement initiated by the Dutch, but with their own set of policies and strategies. The British colonial administration implemented legal frameworks that formalised the control of land and resources, often disregarding indigenous land tenure systems and further entrenching colonial control.

The combination of Dutch and British policies resulted In a systematic and widespread dispossession of indigenous lands across South Africa. The introduction of European land ownership concepts, combined with military and legal measures, led to the marginalisation and displacement of indigenous communities. These processes not only disrupted traditional land management systems but also had lasting socio-economic and cultural impacts on the affected populations.[59]

The establishment of Dutch settlements introduced new land management practices that were fundamentally different from those of the indigenous communities. The European approach to land use was driven by notions of private property and economic exploitation, which contrasted sharply with the communal and spiritually integrated systems of land management practiced by the indigenous peoples. The imposition of European land tenure systems disrupted traditional practices and led to the marginalisation of indigenous land management methods.[60]

The British Empire's takeover of the Cape Colony In 1806 further entrenched these injustices. British colonial policies prioritised European interests and facilitated the expansion of settler agriculture and land ownership. Indigenous peoples were systematically displaced from their ancestral lands, which were redistributed to settlers. This period saw the implementation of laws and practices designed to solidify colonial control and marginalise indigenous populations.[61]

The British introduced a range of policies that further entrenched land dispossession and racial segregation. The introduction of land survey

---

[59] R. I Rotberg, *South Africa: The Struggle for a Birthright* (W W Norton & Company 1967).
[60] Ibid.
[61] Ibid.

systems, land registration, and private property laws disrupted communal land ownership and facilitated the appropriation of indigenous lands. The British also implemented agricultural practices that often disregarded the environmental knowledge and land management practices of indigenous communities, leading to environmental degradation and further displacement.[62]

The introduction of the Glen Grey Act in 1894 epitomised the colonial strategy of land dispossession and control over indigenous populations in South Africa. This legislation was a deliberate attempt to reshape indigenous land ownership and management systems to align with European economic and social models, fundamentally altering the relationship between indigenous peoples and their land.[63]

Prior to the Glen Grey Act, indigenous communities in South Africa, such as the Xhosa, maintained traditional systems of communal land ownership and management. Land was held collectively by the community, and its use was governed by customary laws and practices that reflected the social and cultural values of these societies. These traditional systems were integral to the social cohesion and economic stability of indigenous communities, supporting a way of life that was adapted to local conditions and resources.

The Glen Grey Act, however, sought to dismantle these communal systems by imposing a European-style system of land ownership. The Act mandated the allocation of land in small, individual plots, effectively breaking up communal land holdings and undermining traditional land management practices. This approach was part of a broader colonial strategy to assimilate indigenous peoples into the European economic system, which was based on the principles of private land ownership and individual economic activity.[64]

One of the primary objectives of the Glen Grey Act was to promote individual land ownership among indigenous peoples as a means of integrating them into the colonial economy. By converting communal land into privately owned plots, the Act aimed to align indigenous land

---

[62] Beck, *The History of South Africa* (n55)
[63] Glen Grey Act 1894 (56 & 57 Vict c 40)
[64] Ibid.

use with European economic practices, which centred on the exploitation of land and resources for the benefit of settlers. This shift was intended to facilitate the extraction of resources and the expansion of agricultural production in a manner that served the interests of the colonial administration and European settlers.[65]

The Act had profound and far-reaching effects on indigenous communities. The fragmentation of land holdings undermined traditional social structures, which were closely tied to communal land management. Indigenous societies had developed intricate systems of land use that supported their social organisation and cultural practices. The imposition of individual land ownership disrupted these systems, leading to a breakdown in community cohesion and a loss of social capital.

Furthermore, the individualisation of land ownership led to the concentration of land in the hands of a few individuals, often those with greater resources or connections to colonial authorities. This concentration exacerbated existing inequalities and created significant economic hardships for many indigenous people. Those who were unable to secure or retain land faced severe economic challenges, including limited access to resources and reduced opportunities for agricultural and economic activities.

The impact of the Glen Grey Act was further compounded by other colonial policies that restricted access to resources and economic opportunities for indigenous communities. These policies included land tenure regulations, pass laws, and discriminatory practices that limited indigenous peoples' ability to engage in economic activities and access markets. Collectively, these measures were designed to reinforce the economic and social dominance of European settlers while marginalising and exploiting indigenous populations.[66]

The consequences of the Glen Grey Act and related policies were not only economic but also cultural and social. The erosion of communal land management systems contributed to the disintegration of traditional social structures and cultural practices. Indigenous communities faced

---

[65] Glen Grey Act 1894
[66] Ibid.

significant challenges in adapting to the new economic and social realities imposed by colonial rule, leading to long-term effects on their socio-economic conditions and cultural identity.[67]

In the years following the Glen Grey Act, the legacy of land dispossession and fragmentation continued to shape the experiences of indigenous peoples in South Africa. The Act's implementation laid the groundwork for further land dispossession and marginalisation, contributing to the broader pattern of inequality and injustice that characterised the colonial and apartheid eras.[68]

The Glen Grey Act exemplifies how colonial policies were designed to undermine indigenous systems of land management and integrate indigenous peoples into a colonial economy that prioritised the interests of European settlers. By disrupting traditional land ownership structures and promoting individualisation, the Act sought to facilitate the exploitation of land and resources while marginalising indigenous communities. The profound and lasting effects of the Glen Grey Act highlight the ways in which colonial policies reshaped indigenous societies and contributed to enduring legacies of inequality and dispossession.

The Legacy of the Group Areas Act

The Introduction of apartheid in South Africa in 1948 represents a pivotal and tragic chapter in the nation's history, marking the formalisation of racial segregation and institutionalised economic inequality. The apartheid regime, led by the National Party, embarked on a comprehensive programme to entrench white supremacy, control land, and perpetuate the marginalisation of non-white South Africans. This era was defined by a series of draconian laws and policies aimed at consolidating racial boundaries and maintaining the economic and political dominance of the white minority.[69]

---

[67] Glen Grey Act 1894
[68] Ibid
[69] Nigel Worden, *The Making of Modern South Africa: Conquest, Apartheid, Democracy* (Wiley-

At the heart of apartheid's racial engineering was the Group Areas Act of 1950, which sought to segregate South Africa along racial lines by designating specific geographic areas for different racial groups. This legislation was not merely a tool of segregation but a systematic approach to enforcing racial divisions and reinforcing the economic advantages of the white minority. The Act mandated that non-white South Africans, including Africans, Indians, and Coloureds, be forcibly removed from areas designated as "white" and relocated to areas set aside for their racial group. These designated areas, often referred to as "homelands" or "Bantustans," were strategically chosen to confine non-white populations to less economically viable and less developed regions, thereby consolidating white control over valuable land and resources.[70]

The Implementation of the Group Areas Act had immediate and profound consequences for non-white South Africans. Communities that had lived in urban areas for generations were displaced, resulting in widespread social dislocation and economic hardship. The forced removals were carried out with a heavy hand, often involving the demolition of homes and the destruction of established communities. The relocation to Bantustans not only disrupted social networks but also imposed severe economic constraints on displaced populations. The Bantustans were frequently located in areas with poor agricultural potential, limited infrastructure, and insufficient public services. As a result, the displaced communities faced significant challenges in rebuilding their lives and accessing basic necessities.[71]

The Group Areas Act was part of a broader system of racial segregation that sought to entrench white supremacy and consolidate control over land and resources. The apartheid regime aimed to create a rigid racial hierarchy that placed whites at the top and relegated non-whites to subordinate positions. This segregation was not only geographical but also economic, social, and political. The regime's policies ensured that economic opportunities and resources were concentrated in the hands of the white minority, while non-white South

---

Blackwell, 2012).
[70] Group Areas Act, Act No. 41 of 1950, South Africa.
[71] Ibid.

Africans were systematically deprived of access to land, education, and employment.[72]

One of the key components of this system was the Bantu Authorities Act of 1951, which further entrenched apartheid by transferring administrative powers to tribal leaders under state control. The Act sought to create a façade of indigenous governance while ensuring that real political and administrative power remained in the hands of the apartheid state. By delegating administrative responsibilities to tribal leaders, the regime aimed to consolidate its control over indigenous communities and undermine their political and land rights. The Bantu Authorities Act effectively eroded traditional political structures and replaced them with a system that was subordinated to the apartheid government.[73]

The creation of Bantustans was central to the apartheid strategy of political and social control. These areas were designated for specific racial groups and were intended to serve as a means of segregating and controlling the population. The Bantustans were often situated in economically marginalised regions, chosen for their limited development potential and isolation from major economic centres. This strategic placement served multiple purposes: it prevented non-white populations from accessing valuable resources and economic opportunities, while also reinforcing the notion of separate development.[74]

The Bantustans were characterised by a lack of infrastructure and public services, which further exacerbated the economic disadvantages faced by their residents. The apartheid regime's policies ensured that the Bantustans remained economically dependent on the state, with limited prospects for economic growth or self-sufficiency. The political and economic marginalisation of Bantustan residents was compounded by restrictions on their movement and employment, which prevented them from accessing opportunities outside their designated areas. This system of control was designed to reinforce the segregationist policies of apartheid while maintaining the economic and political dominance of the

---

[72] Group Areas Act, Act No. 41 of 1950, South Africa.
[73] Ibid.
[74] Ibid.

white minority.[75]

The impact of these policies on non-white South Africans was profound and far-reaching. The spatial and economic inequalities created by apartheid have had lasting effects on the socio-economic landscape of South Africa. The forced removals and land dispossession experienced during apartheid have contributed to ongoing disparities in land ownership, economic opportunities, and social cohesion. The legacy of apartheid policies continues to shape the experiences of South Africa's diverse communities, and addressing these historical injustices is crucial for achieving social justice and reconciliation.

The apartheid regime's policies were designed to entrench racial segregation and economic inequality by systematically dispossessing non-white South Africans of their land and resources. The Group Areas Act and the Bantu Authorities Act were key components of this strategy, serving to reinforce white control over valuable land and resources while marginalising and exploiting non-white populations. The creation of Bantustans and the imposition of administrative control over indigenous communities were central to the apartheid regime's efforts to maintain its grip on power and perpetuate its system of racial and economic dominance.

The legacy of apartheid Is evident in the continuing socio-economic disparities and political challenges faced by South Africa. The forced removals, land dispossession, and economic marginalisation experienced during apartheid have left enduring scars on the nation. Addressing these legacies requires a comprehensive approach that involves recognising and redressing historical injustices, implementing policies to promote economic and social equity, and fostering reconciliation among South Africa's diverse communities.

Efforts to address the impact of apartheid have included various forms of redress, such as land restitution programmes, economic empowerment initiatives, and social development projects. These efforts aim to address the historical injustices and provide opportunities for previously marginalised communities. However, the process of achieving social justice and reconciliation is ongoing, and continued efforts are

---

[75] Group Areas Act, Act No. 41 of 1950, South Africa.

needed to build a more equitable and inclusive society.[76]

The journey towards justice and reconciliation Is a complex and challenging one, requiring a deep understanding of the historical context and the ways in which apartheid policies have shaped contemporary South Africa. This journey involves addressing the legacies of apartheid, promoting economic and social equity, and fostering a sense of unity and shared purpose among all South Africans.

Apartheid policies, implemented by the National Party after 1948, resulted in pronounced disparities in living conditions and economic opportunities between racial groups in South Africa. This system of racial segregation and discrimination systematically entrenched inequality and left a legacy of profound socio-economic imbalances that have had lasting effects on South African society.[77]

Under apartheid, land was allocated to indigenous communities in a manner that was both strategically discriminatory and economically disadvantageous. The land designated for non-white populations was often of significantly lower quality compared to the land that was appropriated for white settlers. This land was typically less fertile, less accessible, and often situated in areas with limited potential for development. Consequently, the economic opportunities available to non-white communities were severely constrained. The allocated land frequently lacked essential infrastructure, such as roads, schools, and healthcare facilities, which further exacerbated the challenges faced by these communities.[78]

The segregation policies enforced by apartheid resulted in overcrowded living conditions for many non-white South Africans. The forced removals and relocations, dictated by legislation such as the Group Areas Act, concentrated non-white populations into specific areas that were often ill-equipped to handle the influx of residents. These areas, known as Bantustans or townships, were marked by overcrowding, inadequate housing, and insufficient public services. The lack of proper

---

[76] Shadrack Maake, *Land Reform in South Africa: Obstinate Spatial Distortions* (Thesis, University of Limpopo).
[77] Worden, *The Making of Modern South Africa: Conquest, Apartheid, Democracy* (n69)
[78] Ibid.

sanitation, clean water, and effective waste management in these areas contributed to poor living conditions and elevated health risks. The inadequate infrastructure and limited resources in these segregated areas perpetuated a cycle of poverty and deprivation.[79]

Economic opportunities for non-white South Africans were heavily restricted by apartheid policies. Access to employment, education, and business opportunities was controlled and limited by racial segregation laws. Non-white individuals were often excluded from skilled jobs and economic activities that were reserved for the white minority. The apartheid regime's economic policies were designed to maintain a labour force that was cheap and easily exploitable, reinforcing the economic advantage of the white minority while keeping the majority of non-white South Africans in poverty. The limited economic opportunities available to non-white communities were further compounded by the lack of access to quality education and vocational training, which hindered their ability to improve their socio-economic conditions.[80]

The apartheid system entrenched economic Inequalities by systematically favouring white South Africans in land ownership and resource allocation. The state's policies ensured that the majority of the country's wealth, including agricultural land and natural resources, was concentrated in the hands of the white minority. This skewed distribution of land and resources reinforced a socio-economic hierarchy that privileged whites and disadvantaged non-whites. The economic advantage enjoyed by the white minority was maintained through discriminatory practices and legal frameworks that excluded non-white individuals from participating in the mainstream economy on an equal footing.[81]

The segregationist policies of apartheid also reinforced social divisions, creating a society characterised by racial and economic stratification. The physical and social separation of racial groups led to the development of distinct and unequal living environments, further entrenching social divisions. The economic disparity between white and

---

[79] Worden, *The Making of Modern South Africa: Conquest, Apartheid, Democracy* (n69)
[80] Brian Lapping, *Apartheid: A History* (Macmillan, 1986).
[81] Ibid.

non-white communities was not only a matter of material wealth but also a reflection of the deeply ingrained racial hierarchies perpetuated by the apartheid regime. The stark contrast in living conditions and economic opportunities contributed to a fragmented society where racial tensions and divisions were exacerbated.[82]

The legacy of apartheid's economic and social policies continues to influence South African society. The disparities created by apartheid have had enduring effects on land ownership, economic opportunities, and social cohesion. Despite the end of apartheid in 1994, the socio-economic imbalances resulting from decades of segregation and discrimination have not been fully addressed. Efforts to redress these imbalances, such as land reform programmes and socio-economic development initiatives, have faced significant challenges and have had varying degrees of success.[83]

Land reform, in particular, has been a focal point of post-apartheid efforts to address historical injustices. The aim has been to redistribute land to previously disadvantaged communities and to rectify the inequities created by apartheid land policies. However, the process has been fraught with difficulties, including bureaucratic inefficiencies, corruption, and resistance from vested interests. The challenge of addressing historical land dispossession and economic inequality remains a complex and ongoing issue in South Africa.[84]

Social cohesion and integration have also been affected by the legacy of apartheid. The divisions created by apartheid policies have left a lasting imprint on social relations, with racial and economic inequalities continuing to shape interactions between different communities. Efforts to build a more inclusive and equitable society require addressing not only the material aspects of inequality but also the social and psychological impacts of apartheid's legacy.

The economic impact of apartheid was profound, with many indigenous communities facing high levels of poverty, unemployment, and inadequate access to education and healthcare. The segregation of

---

[82] Brian Lapping, *Apartheid: A History* (Macmillan, 1986).
[83] Lapping, *Apartheid: A History* (n80).
[84] Maake, *Land Reform in South Africa*. (n76)

land and resources resulted in the marginalisation of large segments of the population, perpetuating a cycle of disadvantage that continued long after the formal end of apartheid. The disparities created by apartheid policies have had lasting effects on South Africa's socio-economic landscape, with many communities still grappling with the legacy of dispossession and marginalisation.[85]

Post-Apartheid Land Reform: Challenges and Progress

In the post-apartheid era, the South African government has implemented various land reform policies aimed at addressing historical injustices. The Land Reform Act of 1994 and subsequent policies sought to redress the imbalances created by apartheid By promoting land redistribution, restitution, and tenure reform. These policies aimed to transfer land to historically disadvantaged communities, restore land that was wrongfully taken, and improve land tenure security for those living in precarious conditions. The land reform initiatives were designed to address the deep-seated inequalities in land ownership and use that were entrenched during the colonial and apartheid periods.[86]

The Land Reform Act of 1994 was a landmark piece of legislation that laid the foundation for the government's efforts to rectify historical injustices. It established the framework for land restitution, which sought to return land to individuals and communities that had been dispossessed during the colonial and apartheid eras. Land redistribution aimed to provide previously disadvantaged individuals with access to land for agricultural and residential purposes. Tenure reform focused on securing land rights for those living in informal settlements or on land that had been allocated under insecure conditions.[87]

Despite the ambitious goals of these land reform policies, the implementation has faced numerous challenges. Bureaucratic inefficiencies, inadequate resources, and political resistance have

---

[85] Lapping, *Apartheid: A History* (n80, n83)
[86] South Africa, Land Reform Act 3 of 1994.
[87] Ibid.

hindered progress. The process has been marred by delays, corruption, and a lack of effective implementation strategies. Many of the initial targets for land redistribution and restitution have not been met, and the pace of reform has been slower than anticipated.

One significant challenge has been the issue of land claims. The process for lodging and adjudicating claims has been complex and time-consuming, often involving lengthy legal battles and negotiations. The Land Claims Court, established to handle restitution claims, has faced a backlog of cases and limited capacity to deal with the volume of claims submitted. This has resulted in frustration and disillusionment among claimants and has slowed down the progress of land restitution. Another challenge has been the integration of redistributed land into productive use. Many beneficiaries of land reform have struggled to make effective use of their land due to a lack of support, training, and access to resources.

The lack of infrastructure and services in some redistributed areas has further impeded the successful implementation of land reform. The failure to provide adequate support and resources has led to instances where redistributed land has not been effectively utilised, undermining the goals of land reform.

In response to these challenges, the South African government has explored various strategies to enhance the effectiveness of land reform. This includes efforts to streamline the land claims process, improve support for beneficiaries, and address issues of land tenure insecurity. There have been initiatives to increase transparency and accountability in the land reform process, aiming to reduce corruption and ensure that land is allocated fairly and efficiently.

The government has also sought to balance the need for equitable land distribution with the need to maintain agricultural productivity and economic stability. This has involved negotiating with various stakeholders, including agricultural organisations and landowners, to find solutions that address both historical grievances and current economic realities. The focus has been on creating sustainable and viable solutions that support economic development while addressing the injustices of the past. Community-based approaches have also been employed to address land reform challenges. Various non-governmental organisations and community groups have been involved in advocating for land rights, supporting land reform initiatives, and providing assistance to beneficiaries. These organisations have played a crucial role in raising awareness about land issues, facilitating community engagement, and providing practical support to land reform projects.

Innovative approaches to land reform have emerged, such as the establishment of land trusts and cooperative farming initiatives. Land trusts involve the collective ownership and management of land by communities or groups, providing a framework for equitable land distribution and shared responsibility. Cooperative farming initiatives aim to enhance the productivity and sustainability of redistributed land by fostering collaboration and shared resources among beneficiaries.

Understanding the historical background of land dispossession in South Africa is crucial for comprehending contemporary debates surrounding land reform and expropriation. The history of colonial and apartheid-era dispossession has created a complex landscape of land ownership and use, marked by profound inequalities and injustices. This historical context provides essential insights into the motivations behind land reform policies and the challenges faced in addressing historical grievances.

The legacy of these policies continues to influence contemporary land issues, making it imperative to consider historical injustices when evaluating current proposals for land expropriation and reform. Addressing these issues requires a nuanced understanding of the historical context and a commitment to pursuing equitable solutions that recognise and rectify past injustices. The call for land reform is not merely about rectifying past wrongs but also about restoring dignity, rights, and opportunities to those who have been systematically disenfranchised.

Conclusion

The path towards land justice in South Africa involves acknowledging the past, understanding its impact on the present, and working towards a more equitable and inclusive future. This journey requires a comprehensive approach that addresses both historical wrongs and current disparities. It involves creating a framework for sustainable land management and social cohesion, ensuring that land reform initiatives contribute to long-term economic development and social stability. As South Africa continues to grapple with the legacies of its past, the pursuit of land justice remains a critical and ongoing endeavour. The government, civil society, and other stakeholders must work together to address the complex issues related to land ownership, land use, and land reform. This includes developing strategies that promote equitable land distribution, enhance support for beneficiaries, and address the challenges of land tenure insecurity.

It is imperative to recognise the profound and far-reaching impact of land dispossession and racial oppression on South Africa's history and contemporary society. The legacy of colonial and apartheid brutality represents a dark and enduring chapter, one that has shaped not only the physical landscape of the country but also its social and economic fabric. The radical nature of the violence and systemic discrimination employed during these periods reveals a deliberate and calculated effort to subjugate indigenous peoples and entrench a racial hierarchy that privileged white settlers and marginalised non-white populations.

The colonial era marked the beginning of a systematic campaign of land dispossession and racial exploitation. The arrival of European settlers, first the Dutch and later the British, was not merely an act of exploration or trade but a ruthless conquest aimed at asserting dominance over indigenous communities. The Khoikhoi, San, Zulu, and Xhosa peoples faced intense violence and displacement as colonial powers expanded their territories. The Dutch East India Company's establishment of a supply station at the Cape of Good Hope in 1652 rapidly transformed into an expansionist enterprise, leading to brutal conflicts and massacres. The indigenous peoples, who had long lived In harmony with their land and developed intricate systems of land management, were subjected to violent tactics designed to eradicate their way of life and seize their resources.[88]

British colonial rule continued this legacy of brutality, with military conquests and wars such as the Anglo-Zulu War and the Anglo-Boer Wars resulting in significant loss of life and further dispossession. These conflicts were not merely about territorial control but were part of a broader strategy to undermine and obliterate indigenous political and social structures. The scorched-earth tactics and concentration camps employed during these wars reflect the extreme measures taken to subdue resistance and consolidate colonial rule. The brutality of these actions was intended to reinforce the economic and political dominance of the colonial powers at the expense of indigenous peoples.[89]

The advent of apartheid In 1948 marked a new phase of radical oppression and segregation. The apartheid regime, implemented by the National Party, institutionalised racial discrimination through a comprehensive legal and administrative framework. The Group Areas Act of 1950, for example, was a key instrument of this system, designating specific areas for different racial groups and forcibly removing non-white South Africans from their homes. This legislation was part of a broader strategy to entrench racial segregation and white supremacy, resulting in the creation of economically marginalised and overcrowded townships and Bantustans.[90]

The brutality of apartheid extended beyond the physical removal of communities to include widespread state violence against those who resisted the regime. The Sharpeville Massacre of 1960 and the Soweto Uprising of 1976 exemplify the extreme measures used to suppress dissent and maintain control. Peaceful protests and demonstrations were met with ruthless force, resulting in numerous deaths and injuries. The apartheid government's use of police and military forces to enforce its policies was characterised by a pervasive and systematic application of violence. Political activists and ordinary citizens alike faced brutal

---

[88] David Welsh, *South Africa: The Rise and Fall of Apartheid* (I.B. Tauris, 2009).
[89] Ibid.
[90] Truth and Reconciliation Commission of South Africa, *Report* (1998).

repression, including torture and arbitrary detention, as the regime sought to crush any form of resistance and reinforce its authoritarian control.[91]

The impact of apartheid's brutality was not confined to the immediate violence but extended to the creation of lasting socio-economic inequalities. The forced relocations and the allocation of inferior land to non-white communities led to severe deprivation and a stark contrast in living conditions. The apartheid regime systematically underfunded and neglected the infrastructure and services in non-white areas, perpetuating cycles of poverty and exclusion. The economic opportunities available to non-white South Africans were severely restricted, with access to education, employment, and business ventures controlled by discriminatory policies. The economic and social disparities created by apartheid have had enduring effects, contributing to ongoing inequalities in South Africa's post-apartheid era.[92]

The legacy of colonial and apartheid brutality is evident in the persistent socio-economic challenges faced by South Africa today. The historical injustices and inequalities have left deep scars on the nation's collective consciousness, influencing contemporary issues such as land reform, economic empowerment, and social cohesion. Efforts to address these disparities through various reforms and initiatives have made progress but have also encountered significant obstacles.

Land reform, for example, aims to redress historical land dispossession by redistributing land to previously disadvantaged communities. However, the process has faced challenges including bureaucratic inefficiencies, corruption, and resistance from vested interests. The slow pace and uneven success of these efforts highlight the complexities involved in addressing the legacy of past injustices.

Social cohesion and integration remain challenging in a society still grappling with the effects of apartheid's brutal legacy. The physical and social divisions created by apartheid have left a lasting imprint on South African society, with racial and economic inequalities continuing to shape interactions between different communities. Building a more inclusive

---

[91] Truth and Reconciliation Commission of South Africa, Report (1998)
[92] Ibid.

and equitable society requires not only addressing material disparities but also fostering reconciliation and understanding between groups. The deep-seated grievances and historical wounds need to be acknowledged and addressed as part of a broader effort to heal and unite the nation.

The radical brutality experienced during the colonial and apartheid eras has had profound and lasting impacts on South Africa. The extreme violence and systemic discrimination employed during these periods were designed to assert white dominance and undermine indigenous societies. The legacy of this brutality continues to affect South Africa's socio-economic landscape, with ongoing efforts to address historical injustices and promote equity. The struggle to overcome the enduring effects of colonial and apartheid-era oppression is central to the country's journey towards reconciliation and justice.[93]

Understanding this historical context is essential for addressing the lingering impacts of past injustices and building a fair and inclusive future. The challenges faced in rectifying these disparities reflect the complexity of dealing with a legacy of radical brutality, highlighting the need for continued commitment to social and economic justice in South Africa.

---

[93] Truth and Reconciliation Commission of South Africa, *Report* (1998).

2. LAND EXPROPRIATION WITHOUT COMPENSATION A NECESSITY FOR JUSTICE

Julius Malema's assertion that "We want the land. The liberation of the continent will come from the expropriation of land without compensation through democratic processes."[94] highlights the crucial role land plays in shaping societies and their structures. This statement, uttered in the throes of a struggle for economic freedom, encapsulates a profound truth about the relationship between land ownership and societal inequality. In South Africa, a nation with a history marred by colonialism and apartheid, the land question is not merely about physical space but is deeply embedded in the struggle for justice, equality, and economic fairness.

Historically, land in South Africa has been a symbol of power and control. The legacy of colonial rule and apartheid has left an indelible mark on land distribution, with vast swathes of fertile and economically valuable land falling into the hands of a minority while the majority, predominantly Black South Africans, were relegated to marginalised and less productive areas.[95] This uneven distribution of land has had far-reaching consequences, not only for the economic opportunities available to different communities but also for their social and cultural identities. The forced removals, land grabs, and discriminatory policies of the past have created a skewed landscape where the benefits of land ownership and its associated economic opportunities are disproportionately enjoyed by a small segment of the population.

The land question In South Africa is thus a reflection of broader social

---

[94] Tsepiso Makwetla, 'Julius Malema on land, corruption and media freedom' (TV interview, SABC, 1 May 2019).
[95] Lungisile Ntsebeza and Ruth Hall, *The Land Question in South Africa: The Challenge of Transformation and Redistribution* (HSRC Press 2007).

and economic inequities. It is intertwined with issues of wealth distribution, access to resources, and the legacy of historical injustices. For many South Africans, the quest for land restitution and redistribution is a quest for rectifying these deep-seated inequalities. The struggle for land is about more than just physical plots; it is about reclaiming dignity, opportunity, and a sense of belonging that has been denied for generations.

In recent years, the South African government has made efforts to address the historical injustices related to land ownership through various policies and reforms. The Land Reform Programme, which includes measures for land restitution, redistribution, and tenure reform, is designed to redress the imbalances of the past. However, the progress has been slow and fraught with challenges. Land reform has often been hampered by bureaucratic inefficiencies, corruption, and resistance from entrenched interests. The process has also been complicated by the need to balance the interests of current landowners with the need to provide justice for those who were dispossessed. This balancing act has led to debates about the most effective and fair methods for land redistribution and the role of compensation in the process.[96]

The question of expropriation without compensation has emerged as a particularly contentious issue. Proponents argue that it is a necessary and justifiable measure to expedite land reform and rectify historical wrongs. They contend that compensation is not feasible given the scale of the dispossession and the financial constraints of the state. Opponents, however, raise concerns about the potential impact on property rights, investment, and economic stability. The debate reflects broader tensions between the need for transformative justice and the concerns about maintaining a stable and attractive investment climate.

Julius Malema's words resonate strongly in this context, underscoring the fundamental nature of the land question. Land is not just a resource to be managed; it is a cornerstone of social and economic structures. The way land is distributed and controlled affects every aspect of society,

---

[96] South African Human Rights Commission. (2022). Land reform and human rights. South African Human Rights Commission.
[https://www.sahrc.org.za/index.php/publications]

from economic opportunities and wealth accumulation to social cohesion and cultural identity. For many South Africans, the struggle for land is emblematic of a broader struggle for a fair and just society. It is about addressing the deep-seated inequalities that have persisted for generations and ensuring that all citizens have a meaningful stake in the nation's resources.

The land question Is also closely linked to issues of economic development and poverty alleviation. Access to land is a critical factor in economic empowerment, particularly for rural communities. Land ownership can provide individuals and families with the means to generate income, build assets, and improve their livelihoods. In this sense, land reform is not just about addressing historical injustices but also about creating opportunities for economic advancement and self-sufficiency. The success of land reform initiatives has the potential to stimulate economic growth, reduce poverty, and contribute to a more equitable society.[97]

Furthermore, the land question has implications for environmental sustainability and the management of natural resources. Land use practices and environmental stewardship are closely linked, and addressing historical injustices in land distribution also involves ensuring that land is used and managed in ways that are sustainable and beneficial to all communities. This includes addressing issues such as land degradation, resource depletion, and the impact of climate change. Sustainable land management practices are essential for maintaining the health of ecosystems and ensuring that future generations can benefit from the land.[98]

The struggle for land is also a struggle for recognition and empowerment. For many communities that have been historically marginalised, the fight for land is also about reclaiming their place in society and asserting their rights. Land ownership is a powerful symbol of identity and belonging, and for communities that have been displaced or excluded, the quest for land is also a quest for dignity and respect. The process of land reform is thus not only about allocating resources but

---

[97] World Bank, *Land Reform and Poverty Reduction* (World Bank 2003)
[98] Ibid.

also about acknowledging and addressing the historical and ongoing injustices faced by these communities.

Julius Malema's statement about the centrality of the land question in social and economic structures is a powerful reminder of the profound implications of land ownership and distribution. In South Africa, the land question is deeply intertwined with the struggle for justice, equality, and economic fairness. Addressing this issue requires a nuanced understanding of the historical context, the current challenges, and the need for comprehensive and equitable solutions. The journey towards resolving the land question is a journey towards a more just and inclusive society, where all citizens have a meaningful stake in the nation's resources and opportunities.

South Africa's history of land dispossession is deeply rooted in a series of profound injustices that have indelibly shaped its current socio-economic landscape. Indigenous communities such as the Khoikhoi, San, Zulu, and Xhosa and others possessed well-established systems of land management that were crucial to their cultural and spiritual identities. For these groups, land was not merely an economic asset; it was integral to their social cohesion, cultural practices, and spiritual beliefs. The relationship between these communities and their land was holistic, encompassing not just physical sustenance but also a profound sense of belonging and identity.

As mentioned previously, the arrival of European settlers in the 17th century, initiated by the Dutch East India Company's establishment at the Cape of Good Hope, marked the beginning of a process of land occupation and dispossession. The Dutch settlers, driven by commercial interests and a desire for expansion, began encroaching on territories traditionally occupied by indigenous peoples. This encroachment was not a mere matter of land acquisition; it involved a systematic and often brutal process of displacing indigenous communities from their ancestral lands. The settlers employed a combination of violent confrontations and deceptive treaties to facilitate this displacement. Violent skirmishes, conflicts, and wars were waged against indigenous groups who resisted the intrusion into their territories, while treaties and agreements, often under duress or through deceit, were used to legitimise the occupation and transfer of land.[99]

The legacy of these historical Injustices is evident in the socio-economic landscape of contemporary South Africa. The disparities in land ownership and access to resources have persisted long after the end of colonial and apartheid rule. The process of land reform, intended to address these historical wrongs and promote equity, has faced numerous challenges. While there have been efforts to implement policies aimed at redistributing land and rectifying past injustices, progress has been uneven and often hindered by bureaucratic inefficiencies, corruption, and resistance from entrenched interests.

The struggle for land restitution and redistribution remains a central issue in South Africa's quest for justice and equality. The legacy of land dispossession continues to affect the lives of millions of South Africans, particularly those in rural areas who were most adversely affected by the historical policies of exclusion and marginalisation. Addressing these issues requires not only legal and administrative reforms but also a broader commitment to redressing the deep-seated inequalities that have shaped the country's socio-economic landscape. The process of land reform is as much about rectifying historical wrongs as it is about creating a more equitable and inclusive future for all South Africans.

The apartheid era, spanning from 1948 to 1994, Institutionalised racial segregation and economic disparity through a range of laws and policies, the most notorious of which were the Group Areas Act and the Bantu Authorities Act. These legislative measures were instrumental in entrenching racial divisions and consolidating economic advantages for the white minority while systematically disempowering non-white South Africans.

These laws facilitated the allocation of valuable land and resources to white settlers, who were positioned to benefit disproportionately from the economic opportunities provided by the land. The systemic dispossession of land and resources created a racially segregated society with severe economic and social inequalities. Non-white communities were relegated to the peripheries of economic activity, their access to fertile land and critical resources severely restricted. This segregation was

---

[99] Ntsebeza L and Hall R, *The Land Question in South Africa* (HSRC Press 2007)

not merely spatial but also economic and social, with indigenous communities often left with inadequate and marginal land that impeded their economic development and perpetuated cycles of poverty.[100]

Challenges and Opportunities in Implementing Land Reform in South Africa

With the official end of apartheid in 1994 came the promise of a new era of democratic governance and the urgent need to address the historical injustices of land dispossession. The transition to democracy brought with it an acknowledgment of the deep-seated inequalities perpetuated by apartheid policies and a commitment to rectify these wrongs. Central to this process was the introduction of the Land Reform Act of 1994, a comprehensive framework designed to address the injustices of the past and foster a more equitable distribution of land. The Land Reform Act was structured around three primary mechanisms: land restitution, land redistribution, and tenure reform.[101]

Land restitution aimed to redress the wrongs of land dispossession by returning land to individuals and communities who had been displaced by discriminatory laws and practices. This mechanism sought to restore land rights to those who had been forcibly removed from their ancestral territories, providing them with the opportunity to reclaim their historical connection to the land. The process of land restitution involved identifying and verifying claims, negotiating the return of land or compensation, and implementing the restitution decisions. The goal was to restore not only the physical land but also the dignity and economic potential of those who had been dispossessed. The restitution process, however, has faced numerous challenges, including bureaucratic delays, legal complexities, and the difficulties of reconciling competing claims.

Land redistribution, the second mechanism, focused on addressing the imbalances in land ownership created by colonial and apartheid-era policies. This component of the Land Reform Act aimed to transfer land

---

[100] Group Areas Act 1950, Act 41 of 1950 (South Africa).
[101] Land Reform Act 1994, Act 3 of 1994 (South Africa).

from large, predominantly white landholders to previously disadvantaged individuals and communities. The objective was to promote a more equitable distribution of land, enhance economic opportunities for historically marginalised groups, and address the disparities in land ownership that had persisted for generations. Land redistribution involved the acquisition and allocation of land, often through negotiated purchases or expropriation. The challenge of land redistribution has been significant, with issues such as the availability of land, resistance from existing landowners, and the need for effective support mechanisms to ensure successful land reform outcomes. [102]

Tenure reform constituted the third mechanism of the Land Reform Act, focusing on formalising land rights for individuals and communities living on communal land or in informal settlements. This component sought to enhance land security by providing legal recognition of land rights, thereby improving the stability and security of tenure for vulnerable populations. Tenure reform aimed to address issues such as insecure land tenure, lack of formal property rights, and the challenges faced by communities living in informal settlements. By formalising land rights, tenure reform sought to empower individuals and communities, providing them with the means to invest in and develop their land, and thereby improving their overall economic and social well-being. [103]

The Implementation of the Land Reform Act has been a complex and often contentious process. While the Act established a framework for addressing historical injustices, the practicalities of implementation have encountered numerous obstacles. Bureaucratic inefficiencies, corruption, and resistance from entrenched interests have hindered progress, leading to frustrations and delays in the land reform process. Additionally, the scale of the dispossession and the complexity of land claims have posed significant challenges, requiring careful navigation of legal, social, and economic issues.

The impact of land reform on the socio-economic landscape of South Africa has been mixed. On one hand, land restitution and redistribution efforts have succeeded in returning land to some individuals and

---

[102] Land Reform Act 1994, Act 3 of 1994 (South Africa).
[103] W G Moseley, *Land Reform in South Africa* (Rowman & Littlefield Publishers 2015).

communities, providing them with new opportunities and a degree of economic empowerment. On the other hand, the slow pace of reform, the challenges of implementation, and the ongoing issues of land tenure insecurity have meant that many of the deep-seated inequalities perpetuated by apartheid policies remain unaddressed.

The legacy of land dispossession continues to affect the lives of many South Africans, particularly those in rural areas who were most adversely impacted by historical injustices. The challenge of land reform is not only about addressing past wrongs but also about creating a more equitable and inclusive future. The ongoing process of land reform requires continued commitment to addressing the historical and contemporary injustices of land dispossession, ensuring that all South Africans have a meaningful stake in the country's resources and opportunities.

The apartheid era's Institutionalisation of racial segregation and economic disparity through laws such as the Group Areas Act and the Bantu Authorities Act laid the groundwork for severe socio-economic inequalities that have persisted long after the end of apartheid. The introduction of the Land Reform Act in 1994 marked a significant step towards addressing these injustices, with its focus on land restitution, redistribution, and tenure reform. However, the implementation of land reform has faced numerous challenges, reflecting the complexity of addressing historical wrongs and creating a more equitable society. The ongoing struggle for land reform is a critical component of South Africa's broader quest for justice and equality, requiring sustained efforts to address both the legacies of the past and the needs of the present.[104]

Despite the ambitious goals set forth by the Land Reform Act of 1994, the implementation of land reform policies in South Africa has been fraught with significant obstacles. The intent behind the reform was clear: to address the deep-seated injustices of land dispossession, to promote more equitable land distribution, and to enhance land security for historically marginalised communities. However, translating these goals into meaningful outcomes proved to be a complex and challenging endeavour. The difficulties faced during implementation underscore the

---

[104] Ntsebeza L and Hall R, *The Land Question in South Africa* (HSRC Press 2007).

need for more decisive and well-supported land reform initiatives.[105]

One of the primary challenges was bureaucratic inefficiency. The processes involved in land reform are inherently complex, requiring extensive administration to manage land claims, negotiate restitution, and oversee redistribution efforts. The bureaucratic structures established to handle these processes were often plagued by inefficiencies, leading to delays and frustrations for those seeking redress. Lengthy processing times for land claims and the cumbersome nature of the application procedures impeded progress and left many individuals and communities in limbo. The bureaucratic inefficiencies were exacerbated by a lack of coordination between different government departments and agencies involved in land reform, further complicating the efforts to implement reform policies effectively.

Inadequate resources also posed a significant hurdle to the successful implementation of land reform. The scale of the land dispossession and the extent of the reform required necessitated substantial financial and human resources. However, the allocation of resources to land reform programmes was often insufficient to meet the demands of the task. This shortfall in resources was evident in various aspects of the reform process, from the financial support needed for land acquisitions to the provision of necessary infrastructure and services for newly redistributed land. Without adequate resources, many land reform initiatives struggled to achieve their objectives, leaving beneficiaries without the support they needed to utilise their land effectively and build sustainable livelihoods.

Political resistance further complicated the implementation of land reform. The land reform process was not only a matter of policy but also a highly charged political issue. Resistance came from various quarters, including entrenched interests and political factions that were opposed to the redistribution of land. For many long-time landholders, particularly those who had benefited from the racially discriminatory policies of the past, the prospect of losing land or seeing it redistributed was met with resistance and reluctance. Political opposition also stemmed from concerns about the potential economic impacts of land

---

[105] Ntsebeza L and Hall R, *The Land Question in South Africa* (HSRC Press 2007).

reform, with fears that expropriation or redistribution could disrupt agricultural productivity and economic stability. This resistance was not only political but also social, as communities and interest groups debated the merits and implications of land reform policies, often leading to contentious debates and conflicts.

The Slow Pace of Land Reform

The slow pace of reform was another critical issue. The goals of land restitution, redistribution, and tenure reform were set with the understanding that they would require time to achieve. However, the progress was slower than anticipated, and many of the intended benefits of land reform took years to materialise. The delays in processing land claims, negotiating land transfers, and implementing tenure reforms meant that many beneficiaries experienced prolonged periods of uncertainty and frustration. The slow pace of reform was further compounded by the lack of effective mechanisms for monitoring and evaluating the progress of land reform initiatives, making it difficult to assess the impact of the policies and identify areas for improvement.[106]

Beneficiaries of land redistribution often struggled to utilise their land effectively due to a lack of support and resources. While land redistribution aimed to provide previously disadvantaged individuals and communities with access to land, it did not always come with the necessary support structures to ensure successful land utilisation. Many beneficiaries lacked the technical knowledge, financial resources, and support systems needed to make productive use of their land. This gap in support often led to underutilisation or mismanagement of redistributed land, limiting the economic potential of these initiatives and undermining the overall objectives of land reform. Without access to training, financial assistance, and infrastructure, many beneficiaries were unable to fully capitalise on the opportunities presented by land redistribution, exacerbating the challenges faced in achieving meaningful

---

[106] Ntsebeza L and Hall R, *The Land Question in South Africa* (HSRC Press 2007).

and sustainable outcomes.

These challenges underscore the need for more decisive and well-supported land reform initiatives. Addressing the issues of bureaucratic inefficiency, inadequate resources, and political resistance requires a comprehensive and strategic approach. Streamlining bureaucratic processes, enhancing coordination between government departments, and ensuring the effective allocation of resources are crucial steps towards improving the implementation of land reform policies. Additionally, engaging with and addressing the concerns of political and social stakeholders is essential for building support and overcoming resistance to reform efforts.

Furthermore, providing targeted support to beneficiaries of land redistribution is vital for ensuring the success of land reform initiatives. This support can take various forms, including technical assistance, financial aid, and access to infrastructure and services. By addressing the gaps in support and resources, it is possible to empower beneficiaries to make productive use of their land and contribute to the broader goals of land reform. Ensuring that land reform initiatives are accompanied by robust support mechanisms and monitoring systems can help to maximise their impact and achieve the desired outcomes.

The implementation of land reform policies in South Africa has faced significant obstacles, including bureaucratic inefficiencies, inadequate resources, political resistance, and slow progress. These challenges have highlighted the complexities of addressing historical injustices and achieving equitable land distribution. To overcome these obstacles and achieve the goals of land reform, it is essential to adopt a more strategic and well-supported approach. By addressing the root causes of inefficiency, securing adequate resources, engaging with political and social stakeholders, and providing targeted support to beneficiaries, it is possible to enhance the effectiveness of land reform initiatives and work towards a more equitable and inclusive society. The journey towards achieving meaningful land reform is ongoing, and it requires continued commitment and effort to address the legacy of dispossession and build a more just and equitable future for all South Africans.

The concept of land expropriation without compensation has

emerged as a highly debated solution aimed at accelerating land reform and addressing enduring socio-economic inequalities in South Africa. This proposal is grounded in the belief that traditional compensation mechanisms for expropriated land would not only perpetuate historical inequities but also impose an undue financial burden on the state. Advocates argue that compensating current landowners could drain resources away from other critical areas such as education, healthcare, and infrastructure development. The idea behind land expropriation without compensation is that it could serve as a more effective means of dismantling the vestiges of apartheid and colonialism that continue to shape South Africa's socio-economic landscape.

South Africa's current land ownership patterns are a stark reflection of historical imbalances. The legacy of apartheid and colonialism has resulted in a situation where a small, predominantly white minority controls a disproportionate share of the country's land. This concentration of land ownership is not merely a historical artefact but a persistent reality that continues to reinforce economic disparities and limit opportunities for the majority of South Africans. The vast majority of land remains in the hands of a minority, contributing to ongoing socio-economic inequalities that disproportionately affect individuals from previously disadvantaged backgrounds.[107]

Supporters of land expropriation without compensation argue that traditional compensation mechanisms would only serve to entrench these historical imbalances. The financial costs associated with compensating current landowners for expropriated land are seen as substantial and potentially prohibitive. Proponents assert that these costs could divert essential resources away from other pressing needs, including investments in education, healthcare, and infrastructure. Given the scale of historical dispossession and the extensive land reform required, proponents argue that the state cannot afford to bear the financial burden of compensation without compromising other critical development areas.

By removing the financial obstacle of compensation, supporters of

---

[107] Ntsebeza L and Hall R, *The Land Question in South Africa* (HSRC Press 2007)

land expropriation without compensation believe that the government could facilitate more rapid and equitable land redistribution. They argue that this policy would enable the state to address the land needs of disadvantaged communities more effectively and promote broader economic empowerment. The removal of compensation costs is viewed as a way to streamline the land reform process, allowing for a more direct and immediate redistribution of land. This, in turn, could help to address historical grievances and create opportunities for previously marginalised groups, contributing to a more just and equitable society.

The case for land expropriation without compensation Is also framed as a necessary measure to rectify the deep-seated injustices rooted in South Africa's past. The current land ownership patterns are seen as an extension of the inequities perpetuated by apartheid and colonialism. Expropriating land without compensation is viewed as a corrective action that aims to dismantle these entrenched inequities and promote social justice. Supporters contend that such a policy would not only address historical injustices but also create a more equitable distribution of resources, paving the way for greater economic and social inclusion.[108]

However, the concept of land expropriation without compensation is not without controversy and challenges. Critics argue that the policy could have significant implications for property rights and economic stability. Concerns have been raised about the potential impact on investor confidence, property values, and the broader economic environment. The notion of expropriating land without compensation challenges traditional notions of property rights and could lead to legal and economic uncertainties. Critics also highlight the need for careful implementation to avoid potential negative consequences and ensure that the policy achieves its intended goals without unintended repercussions.

While land expropriation without compensation is seen by a majority as a necessary and justifiable measure, others argue that it may not be the

---

[108] Tembeka Ngcukaitobi, *The Land Is Ours: South Africa's First Black Lawyers and the Birth of Constitutionalism* (Penguin Random House, 2018).

most effective or sustainable approach to land reform. The success of land reform initiatives depends not only on the mechanisms used but also on the broader context of implementation. Ensuring that land reform policies are accompanied by robust support structures, effective governance, and clear legal frameworks is crucial for achieving meaningful outcomes. Critics suggest that a more nuanced approach, incorporating elements of compensation alongside other measures, might better balance the need for justice with the practicalities of implementation.

Additionally, the potential for legal challenges and disputes over expropriated land poses another significant concern. Expropriation without compensation could lead to a surge in legal disputes as affected parties contest the decisions and seek redress. These disputes could exacerbate uncertainties in the land market and create a contentious environment that might further impede economic development. The lack of clear and predictable legal frameworks could undermine investor confidence, creating an environment of instability and unpredictability that deters investment and economic activity.

The practical implementation of land expropriation without compensation is also a subject of debate. Critics highlight the risk of mismanagement, corruption, and inefficiencies in land allocation processes. The concern is that without adequate oversight and effective management, the intended benefits of land reform might be undermined. Issues such as fraudulent practices, biased allocation, and lack of proper planning could perpetuate existing inequalities rather than resolving them. These practical challenges necessitate a robust approach to ensure that land reform is implemented effectively and equitably.

Addressing these criticisms involves demonstrating how land expropriation without compensation can be implemented effectively while mitigating potential risks. A crucial aspect of this is ensuring transparency and fairness in the expropriation process. By establishing clear criteria for expropriation and implementing robust legal frameworks, the government can protect property rights while advancing land reform. Transparent processes and legal safeguards are essential for maintaining investor confidence and providing stability in the land reform environment. Ensuring that expropriation decisions are made based on objective criteria and with appropriate legal oversight can help to mitigate concerns about the erosion of property rights and maintain a stable investment climate.

Strategic Planning for Economic Stability in Land Expropriation

To manage potential economic instability associated with land expropriation, strategic planning and support mechanisms are necessary. Developing comprehensive land reform policies that include support for new landowners, such as access to credit, technical assistance, and infrastructure, can enhance the productivity and profitability of newly allocated land. By addressing the needs of new landowners and providing the necessary resources and support, the government can promote successful land use and mitigate the risk of reduced agricultural productivity. This approach not only helps to realise the goals of land reform but also supports economic development and stability.

Addressing concerns about the effectiveness of land redistribution programmes requires a commitment to improving implementation and management. Ensuring that land reform policies are accompanied by strong administrative support, anti-corruption measures, and effective monitoring can help to tackle potential inefficiencies and challenges. Establishing mechanisms for oversight and accountability is crucial for ensuring that land reform initiatives are carried out fairly and transparently. By prioritising transparency, accountability, and support for beneficiaries, the risks of mismanagement and corruption can be mitigated, and the benefits of land reform can be realised more effectively.

Moreover, engaging with stakeholders and fostering dialogue around land reform is essential for addressing resistance and building consensus. By involving affected communities, landowners, and other stakeholders in the reform process, the government can address concerns, gather input, and build support for the policy. This inclusive approach can help to create a more balanced and equitable land reform process, ensuring that the needs and perspectives of all parties are considered.

Despite the critics' concerns, proponents of land expropriation without compensation argue that the long-term benefits could outweigh these immediate risks. They assert that addressing historical land injustices through equitable land distribution can foster a more inclusive and robust economy. The redistribution of land to previously disadvantaged communities is seen as a means to rectify the imbalances created by centuries of colonial and apartheid-era policies. By reallocating land to those who have historically been marginalised, the policy aims to create new opportunities for economic participation and growth.

Redistributing land can potentially lead to increased agricultural productivity. New landowners who receive land through expropriation might engage in farming and other productive activities, which could enhance food security and boost rural economies. Improved agricultural output can contribute to broader economic growth, supporting not only the livelihoods of new landowners but also the stability of the agricultural sector. In addition, increased productivity can lead to expanded access to markets, both domestic and international, fostering economic integration and generating new revenue streams for previously disadvantaged communities.[109]

Increased agricultural activity can also have positive effects on local economies. As new landowners invest in their land, they might create job opportunities and stimulate local businesses, contributing to overall economic development. This expanded economic activity can help address some of the socio-economic disparities that have persisted due to historical land injustices. By empowering previously marginalised communities with land and resources, the policy can promote economic self-sufficiency and resilience, leading to more balanced and sustainable economic development.

The impact of land expropriation without compensation on

---

[109] Ngcukaitobi, Tembeka. *Land Matters: South Africa's Failed Reforms and the Road Ahead.* (Penguin Random House, 2021).

community well-being is another crucial consideration. Land has significant cultural and social value beyond its economic potential. For many communities, land is integral to their cultural identity, social structures, and traditional practices. Access to land can improve living conditions, provide a stable source of income, and enhance overall quality of life. The policy of land redistribution aims to address these broader aspects of community well-being by rectifying historical wrongs and providing opportunities for economic and social advancement.

Communities that gain access to land through expropriation might experience several improvements in their living standards. Access to land can facilitate better housing, as individuals and families can build or expand their homes. Improved living conditions can extend to other areas such as education and health, as landowners may have the means to invest in better educational facilities and healthcare services. These improvements in quality of life can contribute to greater social cohesion and stability within communities.[110]

However, the success of these benefits hinges on effective implementation of land reform policies. For land redistribution to translate into tangible improvements in community well-being, it is essential that the policy is accompanied by robust support mechanisms. New landowners may require access to resources, training, and technical assistance to maximise the potential of their land. Without adequate support, there is a risk that newly allocated land could remain underutilised or poorly managed, failing to deliver the anticipated socio-economic benefits.[111]

To address these challenges, comprehensive land reform policies must include provisions for supporting new landowners. Access to credit, technical training, and infrastructure development are critical components of a successful land reform strategy. Providing these resources can enhance the productivity and profitability of newly allocated land, ensuring that the benefits of land redistribution are realised. This approach can help to mitigate the risk of land

---

[110] Ntsebeza L and Hall R, *The Land Question in South Africa* (HSRC Press 2007).
[111] Ibid.

mismanagement and ensure that land reform contributes positively to community well-being and economic development.

Long-term development is another area significantly impacted by land expropriation without compensation. Addressing historical land injustices through equitable land distribution can contribute to broader development goals such as poverty reduction, economic empowerment, and social justice. Land reform can help to create a more balanced economic environment by redistributing land from a few large landholders to a broader base of small-scale and communal landowners. This diversification of land ownership can reduce reliance on a small number of large entities and foster more inclusive economic participation.

Equitable land distribution can also enhance economic resilience. A more diverse and dispersed pattern of land ownership can help to buffer the economy against fluctuations and shocks. By promoting a broader base of economic activity, land reform can contribute to a more stable and sustainable economic environment. Additionally, fostering innovation and entrepreneurship among new landowners can stimulate economic growth and development. Access to training, financial resources, and technical support can empower beneficiaries to engage in productive and entrepreneurial activities, further contributing to economic resilience and development.

In addition to improving food security, access to land can provide substantial economic opportunities. Land ownership opens the door to various forms of economic activity, including agriculture, small-scale business ventures, and other land-based enterprises. By providing previously disadvantaged people with the means to utilise land for economic purposes, land reform can stimulate local economies and create new avenues for income generation. This economic empowerment can lead to enhanced livelihoods, as individuals and families can engage in activities that contribute to their financial stability and overall economic well-being.

Land ownership often translates into better housing and infrastructure, as people have the means and incentive to invest in their properties. Improved living conditions can lead to better health outcomes, as secure land tenure allows for investment in sanitation, water supply, and other essential services. Moreover, the stability that comes with land ownership fosters a sense of belonging and security, which can positively affect mental health and social well-being. When individuals and communities feel secure in their land tenure, they are more likely to engage in local governance and contribute to community development, enhancing social cohesion and collective well-being.

Infrastructure investments are crucial for enhancing the productivity and profitability of newly allocated land. Effective land use requires access to infrastructure such as irrigation systems, roads, and transportation networks. These facilities enable landowners to utilise their land effectively, manage agricultural activities, and transport their produce to markets. Improved infrastructure can also facilitate access to resources and services, further supporting economic development and market integration.

Educational initiatives play a vital role in supporting land reform by equipping beneficiaries with the knowledge and skills needed to manage their land and engage in productive activities. Education and training programs can help new landowners develop their capabilities, understand sustainable farming practices, and participate effectively in local economic activities. By investing in education, land reform can empower individuals and communities to maximise the potential of their land and contribute to broader socio-economic development.

Addressing the complementary needs of land reform also involves ensuring that support services are in place to assist beneficiaries in overcoming initial challenges and realising the full potential of their land. This includes providing access to technical support, resources, and infrastructure that can help new landowners overcome barriers and achieve success. A well-rounded approach to land reform that integrates these elements can enhance the overall impact and sustainability of the policy.

Learning from Global Land Reform Experiences

Examining international experiences with land expropriation and reform provides valuable insights into the potential benefits and challenges associated with such policies. By learning from the successes and setbacks of other countries, South Africa can refine its approach to land reform and address potential obstacles more effectively.

One notable case is Zimbabwe's land reform programme, which began in the early 2000s. The programme was aimed at addressing historical land injustices by redistributing land from white commercial farmers to black Zimbabweans. The intention was to rectify long-standing inequities and achieve greater land equity. In theory, this approach promised to address the imbalances created by colonial and racial policies, providing previously disadvantaged communities with access to productive land and opportunities for economic advancement.

However, the implementation of Zimbabwe's land reform programme was fraught with challenges. One of the major issues was the abrupt and often chaotic manner in which the expropriation was carried out. The process lacked a clear, structured plan and was characterised by sporadic and sometimes violent land seizures. This lack of organisation created significant uncertainty and instability, which had severe repercussions for the agricultural sector and the broader economy. Many of the new landowners, who were often not equipped with the necessary skills or resources, struggled to manage the land effectively.[112]

The absence of comprehensive support systems for new landowners further exacerbated the problems. Effective land reform requires more than just transferring land ownership; it necessitates a robust support system to ensure that beneficiaries can utilise the land productively. In Zimbabwe, the new landowners often lacked access to critical resources such as credit, agricultural inputs, and technical assistance. This deficiency in support led to a sharp decline in agricultural productivity,

---

[112] "Fast Track Land Reform in Zimbabwe" *Zimbabwe* vol 14, no 1 (A) (March 2002) accessed 21 August 2022
https://www.hrw.org/legacy/reports/2002/zimbabwe/index.htm#TopOfPage.

as many of the newly allocated lands were left underutilised or mismanaged. The decline in agricultural output not only affected the livelihoods of the new landowners but also had broader economic implications, contributing to economic instability and food shortages.[113]

The economic repercussions of Zimbabwe's land reform programme were significant. The decline in agricultural productivity, coupled with political and economic instability, led to severe consequences for the national economy. Zimbabwe experienced hyperinflation, a collapse in economic growth, and widespread poverty. The situation underscored the importance of careful planning and the need for a well-structured support system in any land reform programme. Without adequate support, the benefits of land redistribution can be undermined, and the intended goals of rectifying historical injustices and promoting equity may not be realised.[114]

South Africa's approach to land expropriation without compensation must take these lessons into account to avoid similar pitfalls. While the intention behind land expropriation without compensation is to address historical land injustices and promote greater equity, the implementation of such a policy requires meticulous planning and a comprehensive support system. To ensure the success of land reform, South Africa must address several key factors as mentioned earlier.

Firstly, South Africa must develop a clear and structured plan for land expropriation. This plan should outline the criteria for expropriation, the processes involved, and the mechanisms for ensuring that land is distributed fairly and effectively. A well-defined plan can help to minimise uncertainty and instability, providing a stable environment for both landowners and investors.

Secondly, it is essential to establish robust support systems for new landowners. This includes providing access to resources such as credit, agricultural inputs, and technical assistance. Support systems should be designed to address the specific needs of new landowners, helping them

---

[113] "Fast Track Land Reform in Zimbabwe" Zimbabwe vol 14 no 1 (A) (March 2002) https://www.hrw.org/legacy/reports/2002/zimbabwe/index.htm accessed 21 August 2022.
[114] Ibid.

to manage their land effectively and improve productivity. Training programs and extension services can equip beneficiaries with the skills and knowledge required for successful land management. Additionally, investments in infrastructure, such as irrigation systems and transportation networks, can enhance the productivity of redistributed land and facilitate market access.

Thirdly, South Africa should ensure that land reform policies are accompanied by measures to promote economic stability and development. This includes developing strategies to support agricultural productivity, foster economic growth, and address potential disruptions caused by land expropriation. Comprehensive planning and strategic support can help to mitigate the risks associated with land reform and promote positive outcomes for both landowners and the broader economy.

Examining international experiences with land expropriation and reform provides a deeper understanding of the complexities involved in such policies and their potential impacts. Various countries have implemented land reform in different ways, offering valuable lessons for South Africa as it considers its approach to land expropriation without compensation. Brazil, Namibia, China, and Colombia provide illustrative examples of how land reform can be approached and what can be learned from their successes and challenges.

Brazil's land reform efforts have been multifaceted and nuanced, reflecting a comprehensive approach to addressing land distribution issues. The Brazilian government has implemented several key policies aimed at supporting land reform, including land acquisition programmes, access to credit, and technical assistance. These efforts are designed to correct historical inequities and provide previously disadvantaged populations with access to productive land.[115]

One central component of Brazil's approach is its land acquisition programmes, which involve purchasing land from large landholders and redistributing it to landless or marginalised farmers. This policy aims to

---

[115] Andersen L, Granger C, Reis E, Weinhold D, and Wunder S, *The Dynamics of Deforestation and Economic Growth in the Brazilian Amazon* (Cambridge University Press 2003).

address the legacy of historical land concentration and provide opportunities for economic advancement to those who have been historically excluded. The Brazilian government's willingness to invest in these programmes demonstrates a commitment to rectifying social and economic imbalances through land reform.[116]

In addition to land acquisition, Brazil places significant emphasis on providing access to credit for new landowners. Land reform often presents financial challenges for beneficiaries, who may lack the resources necessary to develop their land effectively. By facilitating access to credit, the Brazilian government helps mitigate these challenges, enabling new landowners to invest in necessary inputs such as seeds, fertilizers, and equipment. This financial support is crucial for fostering agricultural productivity and ensuring that redistributed land can be used effectively.[117]

Technical assistance is another critical aspect of Brazil's land reform strategy. The government provides training and support to new landowners to help them manage their land effectively. This assistance includes guidance on modern farming techniques, pest management, and sustainable agricultural practices. By equipping beneficiaries with the knowledge and skills they need, Brazil enhances the productivity of redistributed land and contributes to broader economic growth.[118]

Brazil's experience underscores the importance of a holistic approach to land reform. Successful land reform requires more than merely redistributing land; it necessitates integrating land distribution with broader economic and social development efforts. By combining land acquisition, financial support, and technical assistance, Brazil's approach helps ensure that beneficiaries can make the most of their land and contribute to sustainable economic development.[119]

Namibia's land reform programme, which began after the country's independence in 1990, offers another valuable example of how land

---

[116] Andersen L, Granger C, Reis E, Weinhold D, and Wunder S, *The Dynamics of Deforestation and Economic Growth in the Brazilian Amazon* (Cambridge University Press 2003).
[117] Ibid.
[118] Ibid.
[119] Ibid.

reform can be implemented effectively. Namibia's approach has focused on addressing historical injustices and promoting equitable land distribution through a combination of land redistribution and tenure reform. The government has prioritise support for previously disadvantaged communities as a central element of its land reform strategy.[120]

In Namibia, land redistribution involves transferring land from large-scale commercial farmers to communities that were historically excluded from land ownership. This process aims to correct historical imbalances and provide opportunities for previously disadvantaged groups. In addition to redistribution, Namibia has implemented tenure reform to improve land security for those living on communal land. Tenure reform provides legal recognition and formalised land rights, enabling landholders to invest in and manage their land more effectively.[121]

Namibia's experience highlights the importance of balancing land reform with efforts to improve agricultural productivity and rural development. The government's commitment to supporting land reform beneficiaries through various initiatives, such as training and infrastructure development, has been crucial in ensuring the programme's effectiveness. By addressing both land distribution and broader rural development needs, Namibia's approach fosters sustainable development and enhances the success of land reform.[122]

China's land reform policies, initiated in the late 20th century, provide additional insights into the implementation of land reform. China's approach has included both land redistribution and tenure reform, with a strong focus on improving land tenure security for rural households and boosting agricultural productivity. The Chinese government's land reform efforts have been characterised by a gradual, phased approach, which allows for careful planning and adaptation.[123]

China's experience underscores the value of integrating land reform with broader economic development strategies. By focusing on

---

[120] Pankhurst, Dawn, *A Resolvable Conflict? The Politics of Land in Namibia* (Ph.D. thesis, University of Bradford 1996).
[121] Ibid.
[122] Ibid.
[123] LL Hin, *Urban Land Reform in China* (Palgrave Macmillan 1999).

improving land tenure security and investing in rural development, China's approach has led to significant gains in agricultural productivity and economic growth. The phased, well-supported nature of China's land reform process provides a valuable model for other countries seeking to implement effective and sustainable land reform policies.[124]

Colombia's land reform efforts are shaped by the context of a prolonged internal conflict, which has influenced the country's approach to land redistribution and property rights. The Colombian government has implemented various initiatives to support land redistribution and strengthen property rights for vulnerable populations, particularly those affected by conflict.[125]

The Colombian experience highlights the importance of combining land reform with efforts to resolve underlying conflicts and support affected communities. Successful land reform in this context requires not only the redistribution of land but also a comprehensive strategy that addresses the root causes of conflict and promotes social cohesion. By integrating land reform with peacebuilding efforts, Colombia's approach demonstrates the potential for land reform to contribute to long-term social stability and development.[126]

Conclusion

Lasty, The debate around land expropriation without compensation in South Africa has evolved into one of the most pressing and contentious issues in the post-apartheid era. The idea of redistributing land to redress historical injustices is central to creating a more equitable society. The need for justice is not only moral but also economic, as the issue of land ownership speaks directly to the entrenched socio-economic inequalities that continue to plague South Africa.

The concept of expropriation without compensation has long been

---

[124] LL Hin, *Urban Land Reform in China* (Palgrave Macmillan 1999)
[125] Ernest Duff, *Agrarian Reform in Colombia* (Praeger 1968).
[126] Ibid.

perceived as a radical move by certain segments of society, particularly by those who stand to lose land, most of whom are white landowners who benefited from apartheid-era land policies. The notion that land redistribution is theft is deeply ingrained in these communities, many of whom believe their land rights are sacred and protected under the law. However, this perspective ignores the fundamental truth that the land was initially taken by force from the indigenous population, leaving them dispossessed and marginalised for centuries.

South Africa's land reform policies since 1994 have been widely criticised for their slow pace and limited impact. The willing-buyer, willing-seller model has failed to deliver meaningful change, with vast tracts of land remaining in the hands of the minority, while the majority languishes in poverty and landlessness. This imbalance not only perpetuates inequality but also threatens the fragile social fabric of the nation. Without drastic measures, the economic disparities caused by land dispossession will continue to sow discontent, potentially leading to greater unrest and instability.

Land expropriation without compensation must be understood as a necessary step towards achieving genuine transformation. It represents not just the reclamation of physical space but also the restoration of dignity for those who have been historically oppressed. The current legal framework, specifically Section 25 of the Constitution, was initially designed to protect property rights, but it also recognises the need for land reform. Amending this section to allow for expropriation without compensation is, therefore, a step toward addressing the historical injustices of colonialism and apartheid, which were founded on land theft and dispossession.

Opponents of land expropriation often argue that it will lead to economic collapse, citing examples such as Zimbabwe's land reform process as a cautionary tale. However, South Africa's approach is markedly different. The focus here is on achieving justice within the bounds of the law and ensuring that redistribution happens in a manner that sustains agricultural productivity and economic stability. The government has been careful to emphasise that expropriation without compensation will not mean the arbitrary seizure of land but rather a carefully managed process designed to ensure that land is redistributed fairly and justly. This framework provides an opportunity for South Africa to implement a more equitable land distribution system that will foster national unity and economic growth, rather than division and chaos.

The economic benefits of land expropriation without compensation cannot be overlooked. By returning land to the majority of black South Africans, the country stands to unlock significant economic potential. The redistribution of land will create opportunities for subsistence farming, entrepreneurship, and local investment, all of which are critical for revitalising rural economies and alleviating poverty. For too long, land has been monopolised by a small elite, with much of it lying fallow and underutilised. By redistributing land to those who have historically been excluded from ownership, South Africa has the opportunity to revitalise agriculture, stimulate growth, and reduce dependence on urban centres, thereby addressing the twin challenges of unemployment and inequality.[127]

It is important to highlight that land expropriation without compensation is not only about economic transformation; it is also about healing the deep wounds left by apartheid and colonialism. Land is more than just a resource; it is tied to identity, culture, and history. For black South Africans, the return of land represents a symbolic victory, a righting of historical wrongs, and the restoration of a sense of belonging in a country where they have long been marginalised. This is particularly important in a society where the scars of apartheid are still deeply felt. The memory of forced removals, broken communities, and the loss of ancestral land continues to haunt generations, and expropriation is a vital step towards addressing these traumas.

However, for land expropriation without compensation to succeed, it must be accompanied by comprehensive support measures. Simply handing over land without ensuring that recipients have the necessary skills, resources, and infrastructure to make productive use of it would be counterproductive. The government must invest in education,

---

[127] Ntsebeza L and Hall R, *The Land Question in South Africa* (HSRC Press 2007).

training, and agricultural support systems to ensure that land reform beneficiaries are equipped to succeed. Moreover, issues such as access to water, agricultural inputs, and markets must be addressed to avoid the pitfalls experienced in other land reform processes.

Land expropriation without compensation is not a punitive measure; rather, it is a corrective one. It seeks to restore balance to a system that has been skewed in favour of a privileged minority for far too long. The land question in South Africa is about justice, fairness, and equality. It is about righting the wrongs of the past to create a future where all South Africans can share in the wealth and prosperity of the nation. The process of land reform, especially through expropriation without compensation, is a bold and necessary step towards dismantling the legacy of apartheid and colonialism. In doing so, South Africa can finally lay the foundations for a truly inclusive and equitable society, where land ownership reflects the diverse makeup of its people, and the sins of the past are addressed with justice and dignity.

3. THE LAND IS RIGHTFULLY OURS "UMHLABA NGOWETHU"

The issue of land ownership in South Africa is intricate and contentious, particularly when examining the indigenous status of the Nguni and other African communities. Central to the debate are contentions made by South Africans of European descent, suggesting that the Nguni peoples—comprising the Zulu, Xhosa, Swazi, and Ndebele—were not originally indigenous to South Africa but migrated from Central Africa at some point. Another argument posits that European settlers arrived on the continent before these African communities had established their presence. Such assertions challenge the historical and legal basis for the Nguni's rights to the land they have inhabited for centuries.

To untangle these contentious claims, it is imperative to explore multiple perspectives—historical, cultural, and legal. Historical evidence, including archaeological findings and oral traditions, is pivotal in establishing migration and settlement timelines. The Nguni peoples have long been linked to specific regions of Southern Africa, with archaeological sites like Great Zimbabwe and Mapungubwe providing evidence of their historical presence and their role in regional trade networks. These sites illustrate that the Nguni were part of a broader historical context involving extensive trade and cultural exchange, predating European contact.[128]

Cultural perspectives further enrich our understanding of the Nguni's indigenous status. The Nguni peoples' rich oral histories, social structures, and traditional practices reflect a deep-rooted connection to the land. These cultural elements highlight the long-standing relationship between the Nguni communities and their ancestral territories. The

---

[128] Peter Mitchell, *The Archaeology of Southern Africa* (Cambridge University Press 2002).

continuity of cultural practices and the significance of land in Nguni traditions affirm their enduring connection to these regions.[129]

The legal dimension adds another layer of complexity to the discussion of land ownership. The South African legal system has long grappled with issues of land rights and indigenous status, particularly in the context of land restitution and reform. The legal framework concerning land ownership often mirrors historical injustices and the pressing need for redress. By scrutinising legal documents, court cases, and legislative measures, we can better comprehend how the rights of indigenous communities, including the Nguni, are acknowledged and contested within the legal system.

Understanding the complexities surrounding land ownership and indigenous status necessitates a nuanced approach that considers various dimensions of the issue. Land ownership in South Africa is not a straightforward matter; it encompasses a range of factors including historical injustices, cultural practices, legal frameworks, and socio-political dynamics. To fully grasp these complexities, it is essential to examine the historical context of land dispossession, which includes the impact of colonialism and apartheid on indigenous communities. These historical injustices have left a legacy of disrupted land rights and deep-seated inequalities that continue to affect land ownership debates today.

Additionally, a nuanced approach requires an exploration of cultural perspectives. Indigenous communities, like the Nguni, have their own traditional systems of land ownership and stewardship that are often not fully recognised within the formal legal framework. Understanding these cultural elements is crucial for recognising the legitimacy of indigenous claims and for designing policies that respect and incorporate traditional land management practices.

The legal dimension of land ownership adds further complexity. The South African legal system has evolved to address historical wrongs through land restitution and reform processes, but these mechanisms often encounter practical and legal obstacles. Scrutinising legal documents, court cases, and legislative measures provides insight into how indigenous land rights are framed, challenged, and upheld within

---

[129] Peter Mitchell, *The Archaeology of Southern Africa* (Cambridge University Press 2002).

the current legal structure.

Moreover, addressing these complexities involves recognising the socio-political dimensions of land rights. Land ownership and restitution are deeply intertwined with broader issues of social justice and economic inequality. By understanding how land rights intersect with issues such as poverty, development, and political power, we can better appreciate the challenges faced by indigenous communities and the broader implications for social equity.

Significance of the Nguni Peoples in South Africa's Land Struggles

The Nguni peoples, Including the Zulu, Xhosa, Swazi, and Ndebele, hold a profound and enduring historical presence in South Africa. Their history is intricately woven into the broader narrative of African civilisation and trade, well before the arrival of Europeans. Archaeological evidence from notable sites such as Great Zimbabwe and Mapungubwe sheds light on their significant role within these historical contexts.[130]

Great Zimbabwe, an ancient city located in present-day Zimbabwe, flourished from the 11th to the 15th centuries. The site's impressive ruins, including the Great Enclosure and the Great Zimbabwe Ruins, showcase the architectural and engineering achievements of its builders. These ruins suggest that Great Zimbabwe was a key player in a vast trade network that extended across Southern Africa. Artefacts found at the site, such as pottery, metalwork, and beads, reveal that the city was not isolated but actively engaged in trade with distant regions. The presence of Chinese porcelain and Persian glassware indicates that Great Zimbabwe was part of a broader network of long-distance trade that connected Africa with other parts of the world.[131]

Mapungubwe, located in the Limpopo Province of South Africa, offers further insight into the trade networks of pre-colonial Africa.

---
[130] Peter Mitchell, *The Archaeology of Southern Africa* (Cambridge University Press 2002).
[131] Richard Nicklin Hall, *Great Zimbabwe, Mashonaland, Rhodesia* (Methuen & Co 1905).

Occupied from the 11th to the 13th centuries, Mapungubwe was characterised by advanced agricultural practices, sophisticated artefacts, and a complex social hierarchy. The discovery of gold artefacts, including the famous golden rhino, highlights the kingdom's wealth and its connections with other trading partners. These findings confirm that the Nguni peoples were not only established within their own regions but were also integral to a wider historical context of trade and cultural exchange across Southern Africa.[132]

The Nguni peoples each contributed uniquely to the cultural and social fabric of the region. The Zulu Kingdom, for instance, rose to prominence under Shaka Zulu in the early 19th century. Shaka's military innovations and administrative reforms transformed the Zulu Kingdom into a powerful and centralised state. The Zulu's social organisation, including their military regiments (amabutho) and governance systems, reflects a sophisticated and resilient society.

Similarly, the Xhosa people, with their rich oral traditions and intricate social structures, played a significant role in South Africa's history. Known for their resistance to colonial expansion, the Xhosa developed a system of chiefdoms and councils to manage both internal and external affairs. Their engagement in trade and cultural exchange with neighbouring communities further enriched the region's cultural diversity.

The Swazi people, with their monarchy and traditional Institutions, have preserved a strong sense of identity and cultural continuity. The Swazi Kingdom's rituals, ceremonies, and governance structures underscore a deep-rooted cultural heritage that has endured through various historical changes.

The Ndebele, known for their distinctive beadwork and wall paintings, represent another vital aspect of the Nguni cultural mosaic. Their artistic expressions and social organisation offer insights into their historical experiences and cultural resilience.

My statement that "Resolving historical land injustices is crucial for achieving equality and justice in our country, as it's essential for genuine national reconciliation." highlights the crucial role of land in South

---

[132] Peter Mitchell, *The Archaeology of Southern Africa* (Cambridge University Press 2002).

Africa's journey toward justice and equality. My insight underscores the importance of addressing historical land injustices to achieve genuine reconciliation.[133]

The historical narrative of land dispossession in South Africa is a deeply troubling epoch that has left enduring scars on the nation's societal and economic fabric. Throughout the colonial and apartheid eras, systematic land appropriation and displacement of indigenous communities disrupted traditional livelihoods and undermined socio-economic stability. These policies resulted in the forced relocation of numerous communities from their ancestral lands, leading to profound and enduring inequalities.

Despite the cessation of apartheid in 1994, the challenges related to land ownership and access endure. The post-apartheid administration has enacted various land reform initiatives to address these historical injustices, yet progress has been sluggish and contentious. The uneven allocation of land and resources continues to exacerbate social and economic disparities, fueling ongoing tensions and dissatisfaction among affected communities.

Land reform transcends mere technical or administrative matters; it embodies a fundamental issue of justice and human dignity. Addressing the historical injustices of land dispossession demands a thoughtful and equitable approach that considers the needs and rights of all stakeholders. Effective land reform should encompass meaningful restitution, sustainable development, and support for impacted communities to ensure that the legacy of land dispossession is addressed in a manner that fosters reconciliation and social cohesion.

The Nguni peoples, with their profound historical and cultural heritage, have made notable contributions to the socio-economic and cultural tapestry of Southern Africa. Archaeological evidence from sites like Great Zimbabwe and Mapungubwe underscores their significance within regional trade networks and broader historical contexts.

My emphasis on the imperative of resolving the land issue underscores the enduring relevance of addressing historical injustices related to land. As South Africa grapples with the challenges of land

---

[133] J Seutloali, 'Speech at the EFF Regional General Assembly' (2017).

reform, it is imperative to acknowledge the historical and cultural importance of the Nguni peoples and to pursue comprehensive and inclusive solutions to the legacy of land dispossession. By recognising and addressing these historical contexts, South Africa can progress towards a more just and equitable future, where the wounds of the past are acknowledged and rectified through meaningful land reform.

The establishment of the Zulu kingdom under Shaka Zulu in the early 19th century marked a transformative period in Nguni history, characterised by profound military and administrative changes. Shaka Zulu, whose reign commenced in the early 1800s, introduced significant innovations that reshaped not only his kingdom but also the broader Southern African region. His approach to warfare, including the introduction of the "buffalo horn" formation, revolutionised military tactics in the region. This formation entailed a strategic pincer movement devised to encircle and overwhelm enemy forces, proving highly effective and becoming a signature tactic of Zulu military campaigns.

Shaka's military reforms extended beyond tactics. He restructured the Zulu army into a highly disciplined and efficient fighting force, centralised command, and established new military regiments. These changes not only bolstered the Zulu's military capabilities but also reinforced Shaka's dominion over his kingdom. His centralisation of power encompassed significant administrative reforms, consolidating governance and establishing a more structured and centralised political system. This centralisation was pivotal in transforming the Zulu kingdom from a collection of disparate clans into a cohesive and formidable state.

Shaka's influence on the Zulu kingdom's expansion was substantial. Under his leadership, the kingdom expanded significantly, extending its influence across Southern Africa. This expansion was achieved through a blend of military conquest and strategic alliances. The Zulu kingdom's interactions with neighbouring groups engendered a complex network of relationships, characterised by both alliances and rivalries. These interactions were instrumental in reshaping the political landscape of the region. As the Zulu kingdom expanded, it reshaped the power dynamics, impacting the political and social dynamics of various communities in Southern Africa.

In contrast, the Xhosa people, who inhabited the southeastern regions of South Africa, encountered their own set of challenges as they engaged with European settlers. The Xhosa Wars, spanning from the late 18th to the early 19th centuries, were driven by disputes over land and resources. The Xhosa, led by figures such as Hintsa and Maqoma, mounted a resolute resistance against British colonial expansion. These wars were marked by significant resistance and strategic efforts by the Xhosa leaders to safeguard their territories and sovereignty.

The Xhosa Wars were not merely conflicts over land; they were also contests for economic and political supremacy. The conflicts underscored the resilience of the Xhosa people and their strategic approach to defending their land against encroachment. The wars were characterised by a series of military engagements and negotiations, reflecting the Xhosa people's determination to preserve their independence in the face of colonial pressures. The resistance efforts of leaders like Hintsa and Maqoma played a pivotal role in challenging British expansion and defending Xhosa territories.

Winnie Madikizela-Mandela, a prominent South African activist, encapsulated the essence of the broader struggle for land and freedom by stating, "Our struggle was a struggle for land, it was all about returning the land to the rightful owners." This declaration underscores the centrality of land in the wider struggle for justice and equality. Land ownership is not solely a matter of economic resources but also a crucial component in achieving social and political empowerment. The Xhosa Wars epitomised this struggle, representing a battle for both territorial control and broader economic and social rights.

The historical backdrop of the Zulu and Xhosa peoples' Interactions with European settlers presents a multifaceted narrative of resistance, adaptation, and transformation. The military innovations and administrative reforms introduced by Shaka Zulu had a profound impact on the Zulu kingdom and the surrounding region. Similarly, the Xhosa Wars illustrate the resilience and strategic efforts of the Xhosa people in defending their land and sovereignty against colonial encroachment. These historical events are integral to comprehending the broader dynamics of land ownership, political power, and social change in

Southern Africa.

As South Africa continues to grapple with the legacy of colonialism and land dispossession, the historical experiences of the Zulu and Xhosa peoples offer valuable insights into the ongoing struggle for land restitution and social justice. The impact of Shaka Zulu's reign and the Xhosa resistance efforts highlight the enduring significance of land in the broader quest for economic and political freedom. By examining these historical narratives, we gain a deeper understanding of the complexities and challenges associated with land ownership and the pursuit of justice in South Africa.

The Khoisan: Guardians of the Land and Culture

The Khoisan, comprising the Khoi-Khoi and San peoples, are acknowledged as some of South Africa's earliest inhabitants. Their profound connection to the land is evidenced by ancient rock art found in the Cederberg Mountains, which provides a glimpse into their spiritual and cultural practices. This art, some of which dates back thousands of years, is not merely ornamental but serves as a profound expression of the Khoisan's worldview and relationship with their environment. The intricate rock paintings and carvings depict various aspects of Khoisan life, including their rituals, social structures, and interactions with the natural world.

The Khoisan peoples' semi-nomadic lifestyle enabled them to navigate and adapt to a variety of landscapes across Southern Africa, from the harsh arid deserts to the lush valleys and mountains. Their extensive knowledge of the environment empowered them to exploit diverse resources efficiently and sustainably. The Khoi-Khoi, renowned for their pastoralist practices, managed livestock and utilised natural resources in a manner that harmonised with their surroundings. Meanwhile, the San, celebrated for their hunter-gatherer lifestyle, demonstrated remarkable skills in tracking and hunting game, as well as foraging for edible plants.

The Khoisan's art and oral traditions reflect their intimate relationship with the land. Their rock art often portrays scenes of hunting, rituals, and spiritual beliefs, illustrating their deep respect for and dependence on nature. These artworks are not merely historical artefacts but are integral to understanding the Khoisan's cultural identity and spiritual life. They offer insight into how the Khoisan perceived their place within the natural world and their role as caretakers of the land. Their oral traditions, passed down through generations, emphasise stories of creation, ancestral connections, and the importance of maintaining balance with nature.

This profound connection to the land underscores the impact of European colonisation on the Khoisan peoples. The arrival of Europeans in the 17th century marked the onset of a period of profound disruption for the Khoisan. Colonial expansion and the establishment of settler communities led to the displacement of Khoisan groups from their ancestral lands. The imposition of new land ownership systems, coupled with violence and disease brought by the colonisers, resulted in significant loss and upheaval for the Khoisan peoples.

The dispossession of land from the Khoisan is a critical facet of South Africa's history of land injustice. The systematic removal of Khoisan communities from their traditional territories laid the groundwork for the broader patterns of land dispossession that would characterise the country's colonial and apartheid eras. The impact of this dispossession has been enduring, with many Khoisan communities continuing to grapple with issues of land rights and access to resources.

In the realm of South Africa's land reform endeavours, the restoration of land to the Khoisan and other indigenous communities stands as a pivotal stride towards reconciliation and justice. The enduring ramifications of land dispossession have contributed to persistent social and economic disparities, making it imperative to address these issues to cultivate a more equitable society. The endeavours to hand back land to its rightful proprietors are not solely about rectifying historical injustices, but also about acknowledging and validating the cultural and historical significance of the land to the indigenous peoples.

The Khoisan's narrative serves as a stark reminder of the broader patterns of land dispossession and the complexities of restitution. Their profound historical and cultural bonds with the land underscore the necessity of integrating indigenous perspectives and rights into contemporary land reform initiatives. The acknowledgment of Khoisan land rights transcends mere historical precision; it embodies a crucial component in tackling the enduring impacts of colonial and apartheid-era injustices.

The process of land restitution encompasses not only the physical return of land but also the revival of cultural heritage and social cohesion. For the Khoisan, this entails recognising their historical link to the land and supporting their endeavours to reclaim and rejuvenate their traditional customs. This intricate process demands meticulous consideration of historical, cultural, and legal aspects, alongside a commitment to addressing the underlying inequalities and marginalisation that have endured for centuries.

As South Africa grapples with the legacies of its colonial and apartheid past, the plight of the Khoisan imparts valuable lessons for the broader land reform movement. The reinstatement of land and acknowledgment of indigenous rights are integral to constructing a just and inclusive society. By confronting the historical injustices faced by the Khoisan and other indigenous communities, South Africa can progress towards a more equitable future, where the rights and contributions of all its inhabitants are recognised and esteemed.

The quest for land restitution transcends mere land restoration; it encompasses the profound cultural and spiritual ties that indigenous peoples harbour with their ancestral territories. For the Khoisan, land restitution signifies an opportunity to revive their cultural heritage and reaffirm their role as custodians of the land. It provides a chance to rectify historical injustices and foster a more inclusive and just society.

In essence, the historical presence and cultural heritage of the Khoisan are pivotal constituents of South Africa's broader narrative of land ownership and justice. Their semi-nomadic lifestyle, extensive environmental knowledge, and rich cultural traditions reflect a deep connection to the land profoundly impacted by colonial and apartheid-era dispossession. The ongoing struggle for land restitution for the Khoisan and other indigenous communities underscores the necessity for a comprehensive and inclusive approach to land reform, one that acknowledges and rectifies past injustices while nurturing a more equitable and just society.

The Bantu Expansion and Its Impact on Southern Africa

The Bantu expansion, commencing circa 1000 BCE, marked a significant migration that shaped a substantial portion of sub-Saharan Africa. This migration facilitated the dissemination of Bantu-speaking peoples across central, eastern, and southern Africa. The introduction of agriculture, ironworking, and novel cultural practices by Bantu migrants contributed to the emergence of complex societies in southern Africa. The Bantu expansion played a pivotal role in propagating technological and cultural innovations, including advanced agricultural techniques and social structures that left a lasting imprint on the region.

The Bantu expansion, which began approximately 1000 BCE, stands as one of the most momentous demographic and cultural movements in sub-Saharan Africa's history. This migration of Bantu-speaking peoples across central, eastern, and southern Africa exerted a profound influence on the continent's social, economic, and cultural landscape. The Bantu expansion was not merely a conventional migration but a multifaceted process encompassing the movement of people, dissemination of technological and cultural innovations, and establishment of new societal structures.[134]

The roots of the Bantu expansion trace back to the contemporary regions of Nigeria and Cameroon. The early Bantu-speaking communities primarily engaged in agriculture, cultivating crops like yams, millet, and sorghum, alongside practising ironworking. These communities devised advanced agricultural techniques, such as iron ploughs and improved farming methods, enabling them to sustain larger populations. The practice of ironworking, involving the smelting of iron ore to forge tools and weaponry, played a pivotal role in facilitating the

---

[134] Joseph Harold Greenberg, 'Evidence Regarding Bantu Origins' (1972) 13(2) *Journal of African Languages and Linguistics*.

Bantu expansion. Iron tools and weapons boosted agricultural productivity and conferred a technological edge in conflicts and territorial expansion.[135]

As Bantu-speaking groups moved from their original homeland, they disseminated these innovations across sub-Saharan Africa. The expansion unfolded over several centuries and involved the gradual movement of people rather than a concerted, coordinated effort. The Bantu migration resulted in the establishment of new settlements and the assimilation of local populations. With their migration into new territories, Bantu-speaking peoples brought along their agricultural practices, ironworking technology, and cultural traditions, which interwove with the existing social and cultural fabric of the regions they encountered.[136]

The Impact of the Bantu expansion was particularly pronounced in southern Africa, where it contributed to the development of intricate societies. The introduction of new agricultural techniques, such as iron ploughs and enhanced farming methodologies, led to increased food production and the proliferation of settled communities. This agricultural surplus supported larger populations and the evolution of more complex social structures. Additionally, the Bantu expansion facilitated the spread of new cultural practices encompassing language, art, and social norms, shaping the cultural landscape of southern Africa.

A salient feature of the Bantu expansion was the interaction and amalgamation between Bantu-speaking migrants and indigenous communities. As Bantu groups ventured into new territories, they encountered and mingled with existing populations. This interaction led to a fusion of cultures and the formation of new societal structures. The process of cultural exchange and assimilation fostered diverse and dynamic societies across the region.

---

[135] Joseph Harold Greenberg, 'Evidence Regarding Bantu Origins' (1972) 13(2) *Journal of African Languages and Linguistics*.

[136] Koen Bostoen, 'The Bantu Expansion' (2018) *Oxford Research Encyclopedia of African History* https://doi.org/10.1093/acrefore/9780190277734.013.191 accessed 19 September 2022.

The migration of Nguni-speaking peoples, including the Zulu, Xhosa, Swazi, and Ndebele, from central Africa to the south of southern Africa is often contextualised within the broader Bantu expansion. However, it is important to understand that the concept of migration in ancient Africa markedly differed from the rigid national borders and delineated territories evident in contemporary times. In ancient Africa, fixed boundaries demarcating distinct communities were non-existent. People migrated and intermingled freely, with the concept of migration being fluid and intertwined with trade patterns, resource availability, and social interactions.

The Nguni peoples' southward migration cannot be construed as migration In the strictest sense; rather, it embodies the perpetuation of the dynamic and fluid nature of human movement and cultural exchange in pre-colonial Africa. The Nguni migration constituted a segment of a broader tapestry of population movements and interactions characterising the region. This migration was propelled by a combination of factors, including environmental shifts, the quest for new resources, and social and political dynamics.

The Nguni peoples' migration southwards led to significant Interactions and integrations with the existing cultural and social landscapes of southern Africa. This period was marked by the establishment of new settlements, adaptation of local practices, and the formation of new alliances and rivalries. These dynamics contributed to the rich tapestry of societies in southern Africa, influenced by both the Bantu expansion and subsequent cultural exchanges.

The legacy of the Bantu expansion and the Nguni migration Is reflected in the diverse cultural heritage of southern Africa. The spread of Bantu languages, agricultural practices, and ironworking technology had a lasting impact on the region. These innovations were integrated into local cultures, facilitating the development of complex societies with distinct social structures and cultural practices.

The Bantu expansion had profound effects on the political and social frameworks of southern Africa. The dissemination of Bantu languages and cultural practices led to the creation of new political entities and the consolidation of existing ones. The interaction between Bantu-speaking migrants and indigenous communities resulted in new social and political structures, shaping the region's historical trajectory.

Julius Malema's assertion that "The land question is fundamental. We are saying that without the land, we are nothing. Our people remain landless in their own country"[137] highlights a crucial issue in South Africa's quest for justice and equity. This statement underscores the deep-seated historical and socio-political challenge that continues to influence the country's landscape and people's aspirations.

As alluded before, in South Africa, land represents more than just a commodity; it embodies identity, power, and survival. The land question is intertwined with broader themes of justice, equity, and restitution, reflecting the nation's legacy of dispossession and inequality. For many South Africans, the struggle for land is part of a larger fight for dignity, recognition, and rightful ownership within their own country.

The historical relationship between land and South Africa's indigenous population has been marked by conflict and displacement. The apartheid and colonial policies created a profound divide, dispossessing millions of their ancestral lands and relegating them to marginalised conditions. The systematic land dispossession during apartheid highlights how deeply land is embedded in the socio-economic fabric of the nation. Forced removals, discriminatory land ownership laws, and racially segregated land allocations have left a lasting impact on the nation's collective consciousness.

Julius Malema's assertion underscores the pressing nature of the land question in South Africa, highlighting its deep-rooted connection to historical injustices. His perspective brings to light the urgency of addressing land reform as a means of rectifying past wrongs and achieving a more equitable distribution of resources. Malema's statement reflects a broader demand for justice, emphasizing that land reform is not merely a policy issue but a fundamental question of equity and reparation for disenfranchised communities.

Malema's stance also highlights the socio-economic implications of land reform. Land ownership is closely tied to economic empowerment and opportunity. For historically marginalised communities, access to

---

[137] Julius Malema, (South African Parliament, 27 February 2018).

land represents a pathway to economic stability and self-sufficiency. Ownership can facilitate agricultural development, business ventures, and other forms of economic activity, contributing to individual and communal prosperity.

The struggle for land encompasses both addressing historical wrongs and shaping a future where all South Africans can thrive. It reflects a broader desire for a just society where economic growth and development benefits are shared equitably, and historical injustices are acknowledged and rectified. Malema's call for action resonates with those who view the land question as a fundamental issue of human rights and dignity, emphasizing the need for recognition and respect for the struggles and aspirations of marginalised communities.

Conclusion

The land reform debate underscores the necessity for ongoing dialogue, negotiation, and compromise. While the call for expropriation without compensation is a significant aspect of the reform agenda, finding solutions that address the needs and concerns of all stakeholders through open and constructive discussions is crucial. Building consensus and fostering collaboration are essential for ensuring that land reform efforts are effective, sustainable, and equitable.

Julius Malema's statement encapsulates the urgency and significance of the land question in South Africa. It serves as a powerful reminder of the need to address historical injustices and work towards a more just and equitable society. The land question is a central element of the broader struggle for justice, identity, and empowerment, and it requires a committed and thoughtful approach to create meaningful and lasting change.

As South Africa continues to grapple with the complexities of land reform, the focus must remain on ensuring that the needs and aspirations of all its people are met. The quest for land is not just about reclaiming what was lost but about building a future where justice, equity, and opportunity are available to all. Malema's passionate assertion highlights the critical nature of this ongoing struggle and the imperative to address the land question with urgency, empathy, and a commitment to creating a more equitable and just society for all South Africans.

In concluding this exploration of land ownership and historical injustices in South Africa, it is vital to recognise the profound and intricate relationship between the indigenous peoples of the region and their ancestral lands. The Khoi-Khoi, San people, Xhosa, Zulu, Ndebele, Venda, Tsonga, and Pedi are not mere historical footnotes but the original custodians of South Africa's diverse and rich landscapes. Their histories are deeply embedded in the land they have inhabited for centuries, and their cultural, social, and spiritual ties to these territories are fundamental to their identities and heritage.

The narrative of these indigenous peoples is marked by a continuous and dynamic relationship with the land that cannot be easily encapsulated by modern concepts of migration and territorial boundaries. Unlike contemporary notions of migration, which are often bound by fixed national borders and defined geopolitical territories, the movement of these groups through southern Africa was fluid and influenced by various factors such as environmental changes, resource availability, and social interactions. In this context, their movement was not a migration in the strictest sense but a natural extension of their adaptable and interconnected existence within a shared landscape.

The profound connection of these peoples to their land underscores the ongoing significance of land ownership in South Africa's socio-political and economic discourse. The colonial and apartheid eras, marked by systematic dispossession and enforced land policies, disrupted these traditional connections and imposed foreign concepts of land ownership and management. This historical disruption has had lasting consequences, manifesting in enduring social and economic disparities that persist today.

The struggle for land restitution and justice in South Africa is not merely about reclaiming physical territory but about acknowledging and restoring the cultural and spiritual bonds that tie indigenous communities to their ancestral lands. Effective land restitution must therefore be grounded in a deep understanding of these cultural connections and a commitment to integrating indigenous perspectives into policy and practice. By recognising the rightful ownership of the Khoisan, Xhosa, Zulu, Ndebele, Venda, Tsonga, and Pedi peoples, South Africa can begin to address the historical wrongs of land dispossession and foster a more equitable and inclusive society.

Addressing these issues requires a nuanced and culturally sensitive approach that respects traditional land tenure systems while navigating the complexities of contemporary legal and economic frameworks. Land restitution efforts must strive not only to restore land but also to rejuvenate the cultural and social ties that the land represents. In doing so, they can contribute to healing historical wounds, promoting social cohesion, and ensuring that the benefits of land ownership are shared equitably.

As South Africa moves forward, it is essential to remember that the land belongs to its indigenous peoples, whose histories and connections to these territories predate modern concepts of borders and property. Embracing this understanding is crucial for creating policies and practices that are both just and respectful, ensuring that all South Africans have the opportunity to reclaim their rightful place within a fair and inclusive society. By honouring the heritage and rights of its indigenous peoples, South Africa can build a future that acknowledges its past and embraces a more equitable and harmonious vision for all its inhabitants.

4. THROUGH THE BARREL OF A GUN: MISCONCEPTIONS AND PROPAGANDA

Since the dawn of South Africa's freedom in 1994, a persistent and often misleading narrative has emerged, propagated by those who either misunderstood or willfully ignored the true essence of the black struggle for liberation. This narrative hinged on the unfounded fear that black South Africans, liberated from the brutal constraints of apartheid, would seek revenge against their former white oppressors. At the heart of this apprehension was the belief that decades of racial oppression and economic exploitation would inevitably culminate in a violent uprising once black South Africans attained political power.

This notion not only underestimated the complexity of the liberation struggle but also misrepresented the objectives of the majority of black South Africans. The struggle for freedom was rooted in a desire for justice, equality, and reconciliation, rather than retribution. Leaders of the liberation movement, most notably Nelson Mandela and the African National Congress (ANC), emphasised forgiveness and nation-building over vengeance. Their vision was to establish a democratic South Africa where all citizens, regardless of race, could coexist with mutual respect and equal rights.

In reality, the transition from apartheid to democracy involved immense efforts towards reconciliation and reconstruction. The Truth and Reconciliation Commission (TRC), chaired by Archbishop Desmond Tutu, was a cornerstone of this process, designed to address past injustices and promote healing through truth-telling and restorative justice. The TRC's mandate was to uncover the truth about human rights violations committed during apartheid and to foster a sense of closure and understanding, rather than perpetuating cycles of violence.[138]

---

[138] Truth and Reconciliation Commission of South Africa Report, Vol. 1 (1998).

The false narrative of inevitable revenge served to distract from the actual progress and challenges faced during South Africa's transformation. While economic disparities and social inequalities persisted, leading to ongoing struggles, the initial transition to democracy was marked by remarkable restraint and a focus on building a new, inclusive society. Understanding this context is crucial for grasping the depth of South Africa's ongoing journey towards equitable and just nationhood.

To fully understand how this fear took root, we must once more examine the historical context of colonialism and apartheid in South Africa. For centuries, the black population was systematically dispossessed of their land, subjected to racial subjugation, and stripped of their rights.

The arrival of European settlers in the 17th century marked the beginning of a long process of dispossession. The Dutch East India Company established a settlement at Cape of Good Hope in 1652, initiating a wave of land seizures from indigenous Khoikhoi and San peoples. This process of dispossession continued with the arrival of British settlers, who expanded their control over vast areas of land, often through violent means.[139]

During the 19th century, British and Dutch colonial authorities intensified their efforts to control and exploit South Africa's resources. The British annexed large portions of land, imposing laws that marginalised the black population. This included the introduction of pass laws and land restrictions that forced black South Africans into designated areas, stripping them of their traditional land rights and confining them to overcrowded and underdeveloped regions.[140]

The culmination of these efforts came with the formalisation of apartheid in 1948 by the National Party government. Apartheid was an official policy of racial segregation and economic discrimination designed to maintain white minority rule. Under apartheid, land ownership and employment opportunities were reserved almost exclusively for the white

---

[139] R. Elphick and H Giliomee (eds), *The Shaping of South African Society, 1652-1840* (2nd edn, Wesleyan University Press 1989)
[140] Ibid.

minority, while the black majority faced severe restrictions. The Group Areas Act segregated residential areas, ensuring that blacks lived in designated townships, often far from urban centres and economic opportunities. The Bantu Education Act enforced inferior education standards for black South Africans, perpetuating their socio-economic disadvantage.

The "White Genocide" Narrative

Throughout apartheid, the government institutionalised racial discrimination, depriving black South Africans of basic civil liberties. Land ownership was central to this dispossession, as white farmers and mining companies controlled the majority of productive land, while black South Africans were relegated to less fertile areas. The economic policies of apartheid ensured that the wealth generated from land and resources primarily benefited the white minority, reinforcing their political and economic dominance.

In essence, the historical context of colonialism and apartheid set the stage for the fear that black South Africans would seek retribution. The systematic and brutal dispossession of land, coupled with decades of racial discrimination and economic exploitation, created deep-seated inequalities that have had lasting impacts. Understanding this history is essential to addressing the myths and misconceptions surrounding land reform and the ongoing struggle for justice in South Africa.

By the time apartheid ended in 1994, the deep scars of dispossession, forced removals, and economic disenfranchisement remained a stark reality for black South Africans. The black population's fight for equality was not only a political struggle but also one deeply tied to the question of land—a source of livelihood, identity, and justice.

The fear among white South Africans, therefore, was not entirely without precedent: they understood, on some level, the injustices they had benefited from and feared the consequences of those actions. This historical awareness contributed to a deep-seated apprehension about potential retribution or radical changes that might seek to redress past wrongs.

As South Africa transitioned to democracy, a palpable sense of anxiety permeated among white South Africans, particularly those with established economic interests in agriculture and property. This anxiety was not merely a result of the new political order but was deeply rooted in a history of racial and economic privilege. For many white South Africans, land ownership was not just an economic asset but a symbol of political power and social dominance. The fear of losing their land was thus seen as a threat to their entire way of life.

The notion of "white genocide," suggesting that black South Africans would seek violent retribution against the white minority, gained traction during this period. This narrative was fuelled by a combination of historical grievances and present-day uncertainties. The historical context of land dispossession and racial discrimination meant that any attempt at rectifying these injustices was often perceived as a personal threat by those who had long benefitted from such inequities.

The fear of retribution was compounded by political and media rhetoric that amplified these concerns, both within South Africa and among international observers. Prominent figures and media outlets perpetuated stories of systematic violence and land grabs, despite the lack of evidence supporting widespread, state-sanctioned violence against white farmers. This narrative served to heighten fears and reinforce the idea that the new democratic government posed a direct threat to white South Africans' safety and prosperity.[141]

In reality, the efforts to address land reform and historical injustices were aimed at creating a more equitable society, not at exacting revenge. The democratic transition sought to reconcile past wrongs through legal and peaceful means, rather than through violence. The persistent fear of "white genocide" thus represented a significant misrepresentation of the true goals of land reform and was often used to resist or undermine these efforts. This tension between fear and the pursuit of justice highlights the complexities of South Africa's journey towards a fair and inclusive

---

[141] BBC News, South Africa: The groups playing on the fears of a 'white genocide' (28 September 2018) https://www.bbc.com/news/world-africa-45336840 accessed 2 November 2023.

society.

Interest groups with vested interests in maintaining the status quo exacerbated these fears by promoting and amplifying these narratives. Their efforts aimed to preserve existing economic and social hierarchies, using the threat of violence as a means to resist changes that might undermine their position. This manipulation of fear not only hindered meaningful progress but also entrenched divisions and perpetuated mistrust between communities.

This narrative was particularly propagated by conservative media outlets, right-wing political groups, and interest groups representing white South African farmers. These entities framed land reform as synonymous with violent confiscation, portraying black South Africans as vengeful and intent on upending the status quo through any means necessary. Conservative media channels, in particular, played a significant role by selectively reporting incidents and amplifying fears. Sensational headlines and exaggerated stories about land disputes and protests created a climate of anxiety, painting a dire picture of imminent upheaval. This focus on sensationalism often overlooked the broader, more nuanced context of land reform efforts, leading to a distorted public perception.

Right-wing political factions and interest groups representing white farmers further entrenched these fears by using them to bolster their opposition to land reform policies. These groups frequently highlighted potential threats and dire consequences, presenting themselves as defenders of property rights and rural stability against a perceived aggressive movement. Their rhetoric included predictions of economic ruin and societal collapse, which were intended to consolidate their political positions and mobilise support against the reforms. The portrayal of land reform as a direct threat to the safety and livelihoods of white South Africans amplified the sense of urgency and danger.

The exaggerated focus on violent land seizures, often reported out of context, significantly deepened fears among the white population. Media reports emphasised extreme cases and isolated incidents, while downplaying the fact that most land reform efforts were intended to be carried out through legal and peaceful means. This distortion not only entrenched the belief in inevitable violence but also contributed to a deeply polarised environment, where rational discussion about the necessity and benefits of land reform was overshadowed by fear and misinformation.

The international community, particularly in countries with colonial histories, also played a significant role in reinforcing these fears. Media outlets abroad often reported on isolated incidents of farm attacks, depicting them as part of a coordinated campaign to forcibly remove white South Africans from their land. This portrayal contributed to a global narrative of "white genocide," despite being factually inaccurate and debunked by numerous studies. The sensationalised accounts and persistent media coverage amplified these fears, resonating particularly with audiences in countries with colonial legacies or significant white populations.

This distorted international narrative found traction in some political circles, where it was used to justify resistance to South Africa's land reform policies. Politicians and commentators in these countries often echoed the exaggerated claims, framing the situation in South Africa as an example of racial violence and governmental overreach. By aligning their positions with the fear-driven narrative of "white genocide," these actors further stoked anxieties among white South Africans and their sympathisers, reinforcing the perception of a global conspiracy against them.

The internationalisation of these fears not only perpetuated misinformation but also hindered constructive dialogue about land reform. The emphasis on dramatic and unverified claims overshadowed the actual goals of land reform, which were aimed at addressing historical injustices through legal and equitable means. As a result, the global discourse became increasingly polarised, with the focus shifting from meaningful reform to defending against an imagined threat, further complicating efforts to achieve justice and reconciliation in South Africa.

At the core of this narrative was a fundamental misunderstanding of the black struggle in South Africa. The fight for equality and justice was never about revenge; it was fundamentally a struggle for dignity, human rights, and socio-economic inclusion. The push for land reform, while central to the liberation movement, was motivated by a need for restorative justice rather than a desire for violence. The reforms aimed to address historical injustices and rectify the imbalances created by colonial and apartheid policies.

Yet, the fear narrative overlooked these nuances, simplifying the complex dynamics of land reform and justice into a racially charged discourse centred on revenge and violence. This reductionist view distorted the true objectives of the reform movement, framing it as an irrational and vengeful campaign rather than a legitimate effort to address long-standing grievances and promote equity. By focusing on sensationalised and exaggerated fears, the narrative undermined the genuine aspirations for a just and inclusive society.

Misinterpretation of Land Reform Aspirations

Contrary to the fear-fuelled narrative of violent retribution, the anti-apartheid movement, led by figures like Nelson Mandela, Desmond Tutu, and many others, was fundamentally focused on reconciliation, nation-building, and peace. This movement aimed to dismantle the system of racial segregation and address the profound economic and political inequalities enforced by apartheid, but it was never a campaign driven by a desire to retaliate against the white population.

The narrative of revenge, therefore, was a gross misrepresentation of the anti-apartheid struggle. It reduced a complex and deeply principled movement to a simplistic and unfounded caricature, undermining the genuine efforts of those who sought to rectify historical injustices through non-violent means. The true legacy of the struggle lies in its commitment to justice, equality, and reconciliation, not in the pursuit of retribution.

Nelson Mandela's vision for South Africa was centred on peaceful coexistence and unity, despite the profound suffering endured by the black population. Upon his release from prison in 1990, Mandela made it clear that the future of South Africa would be founded on forgiveness rather than revenge. He envisioned a multiracial democracy built on shared values and mutual respect, rather than on the basis of past grievances.

Mandela's leadership during the transition to democracy was pivotal in averting the violence many feared. Rather than using his political power to deepen existing divisions, he worked to foster reconciliation and build a unified nation. The Truth and Reconciliation Commission, which he supported, was a key initiative in this effort. The Commission aimed to address the injustices of apartheid through open dialogue and accountability, seeking to heal the nation's wounds and promote a more inclusive society. Mandela's approach demonstrated his commitment to creating a future defined by unity and justice, rather than by retribution.

This desire for justice was consistently misinterpreted by those who viewed the black population's aspirations through the lens of fear and guilt. Instead of recognising land reform as a crucial step towards achieving economic equality and social justice, many white South Africans and their international sympathisers perceived it as an immediate threat to their livelihoods. This misinterpretation was fueled by a narrative of violent retribution that overshadowed the true intentions behind the black struggle.

The struggle for land thus became central to the liberation movement. It was not merely about economic redistribution but about restoring dignity and justice to a people systematically oppressed for centuries. Land was seen as a sacred birthright and a vital link to ancestral heritage and cultural identity. The slogan "Umhlaba Ngowethu" ("The Land is Ours") and "Mayibuye iAfrica" ("Africa Must Return") captured this sentiment, symbolising the demand for the return of land that had been unjustly seized. As I have noted, "The land is a cherished inheritance from our forebears, serving as the cornerstone of our identity and our future."[142] These rallying cries underscored the quest for justice and the restoration of a vital connection to the land and heritage.

The reality is that much of this land was obtained through the violent displacement of black South Africans. The narrative that white farmers had "earned" their land disregards the harsh legacy of colonial and

---

[142] J Seutloali, 'Speech at the EFF Regional General Assembly' (2017).

apartheid-era policies, which systematically favoured the white minority. These policies not only dispossessed black South Africans of their ancestral lands but also entrenched a racially biased system that supported white land ownership at the expense of the black majority. The resistance to land reform often reflects a refusal to confront this painful history and an unwillingness to recognise the need for rectifying these historical injustices.

The portrayal of South Africa as a country in the throes of a racial war, where white farmers were systematically attacked and their land forcibly taken, was both misleading and alarmist. This sensationalism painted a distorted picture of a nation on the brink of chaos, fueling international anxiety and reinforcing the fears of white South Africans. The lack of contextual understanding in these reports contributed to a skewed perception of the land reform process, overshadowing the peaceful and legal approaches being pursued by the South African government and civil society. This international amplification of fears not only hindered constructive dialogue but also exacerbated divisions, making it more difficult to address the underlying issues of historical injustice and land inequality.

One of the most vocal proponents of this narrative has been Elon Musk, the South African-born billionaire who has used his platform to promote the idea of a "white genocide" in South Africa. Musk tweeted about the South African government's plans to expropriate land without compensation, implying that white farmers were being targeted for violence. His comments, though widely debunked by South African authorities and independent fact-checkers, sparked a global conversation about land reform and the safety of white South Africans. Figures like Musk, with significant influence and reach, have played a key role in spreading misinformation about the realities of land reform, stoking fear and division both within and outside of South Africa.[143]

---

[143] Rick Noack, Musk calls South Africa's apartheid past 'atrocious' as Malema leads chants at rally (1 August 2023) The Washington Post https://www.washingtonpost.com/world/2023/08/01/musk-south-africa-apartheid-chant-malema/ accessed 2 November 2023

This international fearmongering has had real consequences. In countries like the United States and Australia, right-wing political figures have used the South African case as a warning of what could happen if land reform or reparations were pursued in their own countries. The narrative of white victimhood, framed as a consequence of empowering black South Africans, resonated with conservative groups that feared similar shifts in power dynamics in their own societies.

The fear of violent retribution among white South Africans can be traced, in part, to the psychological legacy of colonialism and apartheid. For centuries, the ideology of white supremacy justified the subjugation and exploitation of black South Africans, presenting the white population as superior, civilised, and entitled to the land and resources of the country. This belief in racial superiority not only justified the brutal treatment of black South Africans but also created a psychological distance between the oppressors and the oppressed.[144]

As apartheid came to an end, many white South Africans found themselves grappling with the cognitive dissonance of living in a society where the racial hierarchy they had long benefitted from was being dismantled. The end of apartheid forced many to confront the reality of the injustices that had been committed in their name, and for some, this confrontation led to feelings of guilt and fear. The fear of retribution was, in many ways, a projection of this guilt—a belief that black South Africans, if given the chance, would treat white South Africans as they had been treated during apartheid.

Another significant factor driving the fear of land expropriation and violent retribution is the vast economic inequality that persists in South Africa. Despite the political transition to democracy, the economic structures of apartheid have remained largely intact, with the white population still controlling a disproportionate share of the country's wealth and land. This economic inequality has exacerbated racial tensions, as the black majority continues to suffer from high levels of poverty, unemployment, and lack of access to land and resources.

---

[144] Crisis Group, 'Land Reform in South Africa: Fact and Fiction' (2021) https://www.crisisgroup.org/africa/southern-africa/south-africa/land-reform-south-africa-fact-and-fiction accessed 2 November 2023.

The Legal and Peaceful Process of Land Reform

In contrast to the fear-based narrative of violent land seizures, the actual process of land reform in South Africa has been largely legal and peaceful. The government's efforts to expropriate land without compensation are rooted in the constitutional commitment to redress historical injustices and create a more equitable society. Section 25 of the Constitution, often referred to as the "property clause," provides for the expropriation of land in the public interest, with the aim of addressing the vast disparities in land ownership that are a legacy of apartheid.

While the debate over land expropriation has been heated, the process itself has been characterised by legal frameworks and public consultations. The government has made it clear that land reform is not about revenge or punishing white landowners, but about restoring justice to those who were dispossessed of their land. Despite this, the fear of violent expropriation persists, fuelled by misinformation and fearmongering from those who have a vested interest in maintaining the current distribution of land.

Contrary to the fears of violent land seizures, black South Africans have shown remarkable restraint in their pursuit of justice. Despite the deep-seated anger and frustration caused by centuries of land dispossession, there has been no widespread campaign of violent retribution against white landowners. Instead, the majority of black South Africans, including political and civil society leaders, have advocated for peaceful and legal means of land redistribution.

The patience and restraint demonstrated by black South Africans stand in stark contrast to the fear-based narratives of violence and revenge. Rather than seeking to reclaim land through the barrel of a gun, black South Africans have worked within the framework of the law to pursue land justice. This commitment to peaceful resolution is a testament to the principles of the liberation struggle, which sought to achieve justice without descending into the violence that characterised the apartheid regime.

While there have been isolated incidents of violence against farmers, these have been the exception rather than the norm. The vast majority of black South Africans remain committed to the peaceful resolution of land issues, even in the face of economic hardship and historical injustice. This restraint has often gone unacknowledged in the international discourse, which tends to focus on sensationalist stories of violence and unrest.

It is crucial for white South Africans to engage in this conversation with an open mind and a willingness to acknowledge the historical injustices that have benefited them. Rather than viewing land reform as an existential threat, white South Africans should see it as an opportunity to participate in the creation of a more just and equitable society. By recognising the legitimate grievances of black South Africans and working towards a peaceful and just resolution, white South Africans can play a constructive role in the future of the country.

As South Africa moves forward with land reform, it is important to recognise that the process will be complex and multifaceted. There are no easy solutions to the deep-rooted issues of land inequality, and the path to justice will require patience, compromise, and a commitment to the principles of reconciliation. However, despite the challenges, there is reason to be hopeful about the future of land reform in South Africa.

The government's commitment to legal and peaceful land reform, coupled with the restraint shown by black South Africans, provides a strong foundation for the future. While fear and misinformation have often clouded the conversation about land reform, the reality is that South Africa has the potential to achieve land justice in a way that upholds the values of the Constitution and promotes social cohesion.

It is also important for the international community to engage with the realities of land reform in South Africa in a more informed and nuanced way. Rather than perpetuating fear-based narratives of violence and retribution, the international community should support South Africa's efforts to address historical injustices in a manner that is just and equitable. This includes recognising the legitimacy of land reform and understanding the complexities of the process.

South Africa's Constitution is renowned for its progressive stance on land rights, with Section 25 explicitly addressing the issue and providing a legal framework for land reform. However, the interpretation and application of this section have led to intense legal disputes, with various parties attempting to influence its implementation.

The judiciary has generally been supportive of the government's land reform initiatives while remaining cautious. It recognises the need to address historical injustices while protecting the rights of all citizens, including property owners. Landmark cases such as *Agri SA v Minister for Minerals and Energy* have underscored this balance. In this case, the Constitutional Court upheld the government's right to expropriate land without compensation under certain conditions, signalling judicial support for the land reform movement and the legitimacy of land redistribution.[145]

Despite this support, the courts have stressed the importance of checks and balances to prevent abuses of power. The judiciary ensures that land expropriation is carried out transparently and legally, guarding against corruption or political manipulation. The land debate in South Africa intertwines with issues of identity, power, and nationhood.

Conclusion

Let's conclude this chapter by pointing out that the complexities surrounding the narrative of violence and retribution often associated with the struggle for land justice in South Africa highlight the urgent need to confront historical truths. The context reveals that the dispossession of land from indigenous peoples was achieved through brutal means, a fact frequently overlooked in contemporary discussions. Acknowledging the violent history of land ownership in South Africa is crucial for understanding the deep-seated inequalities that persist today.

Fears propagated by white supremacist narratives perpetuate a cycle of misunderstanding and division, obscuring the genuine motivations behind the push for land reform. Rhetoric surrounding "white genocide" ignores the reality that the demand for land reform stems from a legitimate struggle for justice and equality. This narrative serves to instill

---

[145] Agri SA v Minister for Minerals and Energy [2013] ZACC 9; 2013 (4) SA 1 (CC).

fear, promoting the idea that black South Africans seek revenge against their former oppressors. In contrast, the overwhelming majority advocate for redress and the restoration of their rights, prioritising justice over retaliation.

Efforts to amend Section 25 of the Constitution signify a vital step toward addressing historical injustices. This amendment is not merely a legal formality; it is a transformative measure aimed at rectifying past wrongs and establishing a foundation for a more equitable future. The desire for land expropriation without compensation is rooted in a legitimate pursuit of justice, focusing on restoring dignity and rights to those systematically oppressed. This process seeks to ensure that the land, which rightfully belongs to indigenous people, is returned in a manner that upholds justice and equity.

Moreover, the call for land reform is accompanied by a commitment to peaceful and democratic processes. The fearmongering narratives often portray land expropriation as a precursor to violent uprising, overlooking the remarkable restraint and commitment to non-violence demonstrated by black South Africans. The primary objective is not to incite chaos but to engage in a legal and democratic discourse that acknowledges historical injustices and seeks to rectify them through constructive means.

Moving forward, it is essential to challenge misconceptions surrounding land reform and foster dialogue that recognises historical injustices while promoting reconciliation and healing. Land redistribution should be viewed as an opportunity for nation-building, where all South Africans collaborate to create a more just society. This endeavour requires an open conversation about the past and a collective commitment to a shared future.

The path ahead must be paved with a dedication to legal and democratic principles, ensuring that the process of land redistribution is executed peacefully and justly. All stakeholders—government, civil society, and private citizens—must engage in constructive dialogue that respects the rights of all parties involved. The next chapter will delve deeper into the amendment of Section 25 and explore its significance in the broader context of land justice in South Africa, providing insights into how this legal change can facilitate a more equitable distribution of land and resources, ultimately fostering national unity and reconciliation.

5. REVISING SECTION 25 TO EFFECT LAND EXPROPRIATION WITHOUT COMPENSATION

Land reform is often politically sensitive, leading to unrest or conflict when disparities in land ownership are not addressed. By eliminating compensation requirements, the government could demonstrate a strong commitment to resolving these grievances and promoting social justice. This could foster long-term political stability by reducing tensions between landowners and landless populations, and between different ethnic or social groups. Successful land reform could also lead to a more balanced political landscape, as previously marginalised groups would gain economic power and potentially a greater voice in governance, resulting in more inclusive political processes.

Environmental sustainability is another potential benefit. Large-scale agricultural practices tend to prioritise short-term profits, often causing soil degradation, deforestation, and biodiversity loss. By redistributing land to smallholders and local communities, who are typically more invested in the long-term health of their land, the government could encourage more sustainable agricultural practices. With support in the form of access to sustainable technologies, redistributed land could become a model for environmentally friendly agriculture. Such practices would help improve soil health, increase biodiversity, and reduce the carbon footprint of farming activities, contributing to climate change resilience.[146]

The current system of compensating landowners can also be bureaucratically burdensome, with disputes over valuation and legal challenges causing significant delays. By removing the requirement for

---

[146] Kristin Ohlson, *The Soil Will Save Us: How Scientists, Farmers, and Foodies Are Healing the Soil, Saving the Planet* (Rodale 2014).

compensation, the government would be able to simplify the expropriation process, reducing administrative costs and enabling faster land redistribution. This more efficient system would provide certainty for all parties involved, fostering a stable investment climate and ensuring that the intended beneficiaries—marginalised communities—can begin to see the benefits sooner.

From an international perspective, eliminating compensation could be seen as a move towards fulfilling human rights and achieving social justice. Land is recognised as a fundamental right by many global institutions, and equitable land reform is crucial to meeting sustainable development goals, such as reducing poverty, improving food security, and promoting gender equality. A transparent and well-managed land reform process that prioritises marginalised communities could enhance a country's reputation on the world stage, positioning it as a leader in justice and economic inclusion.[147]

Another key advantage of eliminating compensation is the potential to empower women and vulnerable groups. Women, in particular, often face significant barriers to land ownership due to legal, cultural, or financial restrictions. Land reform that prioritises women would promote greater gender equality, enabling them to play a more active role in agriculture, business, and community leadership. Land ownership provides women with economic independence and the security to access resources, credit, and markets, which in turn benefits their families and communities. This empowerment could create a ripple effect, leading to improvements in health, education, and overall well-being.[148]

Under the current system, the requirement for compensation has emerged as one of the most significant barriers to the successful implementation of land reform. The process of determining fair compensation is often fraught with complexity, as the value of the land is frequently contested between the government and landowners. This

---

[147] Sam Moyo and Kojo Sebastian Amanor, *Land and Sustainable Development in Africa* (Zed Books 2008).
[148] Shahra Razavi, *Education for All Global Monitoring Report 2003/4: Gender and Education for All: The Leap to Equality* (2003).

disagreement over valuation typically leads to prolonged negotiations that can take months or even years to resolve. Moreover, the costs of compensating landowners can escalate substantially, especially when large tracts of prime agricultural or commercially valuable land are involved. These inflated costs place a considerable financial strain on the state, diverting public resources that could otherwise be used to support new landowners, improve infrastructure, or develop sustainable agricultural practices.

Legal disputes arising during compensation negotiations further complicate the process. Wealthy landowners, who often possess the financial resources to challenge the government's valuation in court, frequently engage in lengthy legal battles. These disputes can delay land reform initiatives for years, preventing the timely redistribution of land to those who need it most. For marginalised communities that have been waiting for access to land for generations, these delays represent a continuation of historical injustices, further entrenching their exclusion from economic opportunities.

Additionally, the compensation requirement disproportionately benefits those who are already in positions of economic power. Wealthy landowners can afford to hire legal teams to contest compensation amounts, often securing higher payouts through drawn-out legal processes. This dynamic reinforces existing inequalities, as wealthier individuals are better equipped to navigate and manipulate the system to their advantage. Meanwhile, disadvantaged groups, such as small farmers or indigenous communities, are left waiting indefinitely for land that has been earmarked for redistribution but remains tied up in legal and financial wrangling.

The EFF's Motion for Expropriation Without Compensation

By maintaining a system that necessitates compensation, the very objectives of land reform—namely, addressing inequality and redistributing resources more equitably—are undermined. Instead of promoting a more just and inclusive distribution of land, the compensation-based approach often exacerbates existing disparities. It tends to serve the interests of those who have historically benefitted from land ownership, while marginalised communities continue to bear the brunt of the delays and costs associated with the process.

Public engagement and political developments since 2018 have highlighted an urgent and growing demand for a more decisive and transformative approach to land reform in South Africa. This demand reflects a broad consensus among various segments of society, underscoring the need to address longstanding land inequities and historical injustices that have persisted since the apartheid era. The growing support for expropriation without compensation has become a focal point in the ongoing discourse surrounding land reform, revealing both the complexities and the critical importance of this issue.[149]

Extensive public consultations and debates have played a significant role in shaping the current land reform agenda. Across South Africa, communities and stakeholders have expressed strong support for more aggressive land reform measures, emphasising the necessity of rectifying the imbalances created by decades of discriminatory land policies. Public forums, community meetings, and media coverage have all highlighted a widespread desire for land reform that transcends incremental changes, reflecting a collective frustration with the slow pace and limited impact of previous efforts.[150]

Many South Africans are increasingly aware that the legacy of apartheid has resulted in a deeply entrenched land ownership system that favours a minority while marginalising the majority. This awareness has catalysed a demand for transformative land reform that is not only equitable but also addresses the socio-economic challenges faced by historically disadvantaged communities. The narrative surrounding land reform has shifted from merely discussing ownership to a broader conversation about restitution, justice, and the right to land as a fundamental resource for economic empowerment and community development.[151]

---

[149] *Public Parliamentary Consultations and Debates on Land Expropriation (2019).*
[150] Ibid.
[151] Ibid.

Moreover, the political landscape has evolved significantly since 2019, with various parties and movements increasingly acknowledging the urgency of land reform. This shift has led to renewed commitments from the government to implement meaningful changes, including the exploration of legislative amendments to facilitate expropriation without compensation. Political leaders are now recognising that addressing land reform is not just a policy issue; it is a matter of social cohesion and national identity. The public's growing impatience with the status quo is prompting political actors to engage more actively with the demands of their constituents, driving the agenda for substantive reform.

One of the most significant developments in recent years has been the introduction of a motion in Parliament by the Economic Freedom Fighters (EFF). The EFF has been a vocal advocate for land expropriation without compensation, positioning this policy as a crucial mechanism for addressing the deep-seated land disparities that continue to affect millions of South Africans. The motion introduced by the EFF aimed to provide a clear and direct path for implementing land reform, seeking to dismantle the barriers imposed by the current constitutional framework and the compensation requirement.

Initially, the EFF's motion received support from the African National Congress (ANC), signalling a potential alignment on the need for more substantial land reform measures. This support was seen as a promising step towards achieving a more effective and transformative approach to land redistribution. However, the optimism was short-lived as the ANC later amended the motion in a way that significantly limited its scope.

The ANC's amendment to the motion restricted expropriation to unoccupied and "rotten" land, a modification that many viewed as insufficient in addressing the broader issue of land inequity. This narrower focus was perceived as a compromise that failed to address the comprehensive needs of communities affected by historical land dispossession. Critics argued that the amendment was an attempt to placate more conservative elements within the ANC and broader political spectrum, rather than a genuine commitment to transformative land reform.

The amended motion faced strong criticism from the EFF and other advocates for more radical land reform measures. The EFF rejected the revised proposal, arguing that it did not align with the demands for a thorough and equitable redistribution of land. The party contended that the restricted approach undermined the broader objectives of land reform and failed to address the systemic issues that have perpetuated land inequalities. This rejection highlighted the ongoing tensions within South African politics regarding the pace and scope of land reform, reflecting differing visions and strategies for addressing the land question.

The contentious debate over the ANC's amended motion underscores the broader challenges associated with implementing effective land reform in South Africa. The political dynamics and differing perspectives on land reform reveal the complexities of navigating historical grievances, economic interests, and social justice concerns. The debate also highlights the limitations of the current constitutional and legislative framework, which has been criticised for its restrictive approach to land expropriation and compensation.

The ANC has now made it clear that they do not intend to expropriate land without compensation or that they do not wish to expropriate land at all. Critics argue that the ANC's handling of land expropriation reveals an underlying fear of white people.

Learning from International Land Expropriation Experiences: Insights and Challenges

Examining international experiences with land expropriation provides valuable insights into the potential benefits and challenges of implementing policies that allow for expropriation without compensation. Countries like Venezuela have adopted similar measures in her attempts to address land inequalities and historical injustices, offering both successes and lessons that South Africa can learn from.[152]

---

[152] Geo Maher, *We Created Chávez: A People's History of the Venezuelan Revolution* (Duke University Press 2013).

Venezuela's land reform efforts, particularly under the leadership of Hugo Chávez, offer relevant lessons. The Venezuelan government implemented expropriation policies aimed at redistributing land to peasant farmers and cooperatives. Chávez's approach was characterised by a strong emphasis on social justice and addressing historical inequities. However, similar to Zimbabwe, Venezuela faced challenges related to economic instability and inefficiencies in land management. The Venezuelan experience underscores the need for a well-coordinated legal and administrative framework to manage the complexities of land reform and ensure that the redistribution process is fair and effective.[153]

Legal resistance is a significant obstacle to any proposed amendment regarding property rights in South Africa. The Constitution provides robust protections for property rights, and these are deeply entrenched in the legal system. Any attempts to alter these protections may face legal challenges from groups or individuals who view the changes as undermining their property interests. This resistance could come from landowners, businesses, or political entities concerned about the broader implications for economic stability and investor confidence.

To address this, it is crucial to craft a well-founded legal argument that demonstrates how the proposed amendment not only complies with the letter of the Constitution but also aligns with the broader values enshrined in it—namely, the promotion of social justice, equity, and the redress of historical inequalities. By framing the amendment as a mechanism to address the deeply entrenched economic disparities caused by historical injustices, proponents can argue that it supports the Constitution's objectives rather than subverting them.

Engaging legal experts, including constitutional scholars, human rights advocates, and economists, will be essential in building a comprehensive case. These experts can offer detailed analyses that highlight how the amendment is consistent with international legal standards, such as the need for land reform in post-colonial societies, and can provide comparative insights from similar legal frameworks in other countries. Their input will help anticipate legal challenges and bolster the case for the amendment's necessity in achieving a more just and equitable

---

[153] Maher, *We Created Chávez* (n153).

society.

Given that the first round of public participation has shown the majority of South Africans support land expropriation, this represents a significant step forward in the reform process. The public's endorsement adds democratic legitimacy to the proposed amendments, making it more difficult for opponents to argue against them solely based on popular will. However, this support does not eliminate the challenges that remain, particularly around implementation and securing broader consensus among political and economic stakeholders.

With public backing for land expropriation, the next phase should focus on refining the specifics of how the policy will be implemented. Public participation has provided a mandate, but translating that into practical policy requires addressing key concerns. One of these is clarity on compensation models. While land expropriation without compensation may have popular support, a clear and detailed framework is essential to explain how and when this policy will be applied. The government must outline under what circumstances land will be expropriated without compensation while balancing constitutional protections, to avoid legal challenges and ensure fairness.

Another important factor is explaining the economic impact. While the majority supports the idea, concerns may still exist about how it could affect agriculture, foreign investment, and economic growth. The government should now engage the public on how the process will safeguard food security, promote economic inclusion, and maintain investor confidence. Ensuring that people understand the broader economic benefits and protections will be key to maintaining support..

Additionally, attention must be given to ensuring that redistribution mechanisms are fair and effective. With public support for expropriation, the next step is to ensure transparency in the redistribution process, preventing corruption and ensuring that land goes to those who can use it productively. Additionally, providing necessary support structures, such as agricultural training and access to credit, will be essential in ensuring that redistributed land is utilised efficiently and benefits the broader economy.

Fostering dialogue with stakeholders who may oppose the changes, such as landowners and business groups, could reduce opposition. By presenting the amendment as part of a broader social compact aimed at addressing inequality while protecting economic stability, proponents can mitigate resistance and promote a smoother transition towards the desired reforms.To ensure the amendment is implemented fairly and effectively, it is necessary to develop clear guidelines and safeguards. These guidelines should outline the procedures for expropriation, including criteria for determining which lands are subject to expropriation, how land valuations will be conducted, and mechanisms for resolving disputes. Safeguards are essential to prevent misuse of the expropriation process and to ensure that it is carried out transparently and equitably. This includes establishing oversight bodies or commissions to monitor the implementation of land reform policies and address any issues that arise.

A comprehensive implementation framework is also crucial for the successful execution of the amendment. This framework should detail the procedures for fair land redistribution, ensuring that land is allocated to those who have been historically disadvantaged and that the process is conducted transparently. It should also include provisions for supporting affected communities, such as providing access to resources, training, and financial assistance to help new landowners manage their land effectively. Additionally, the framework should outline how to maintain transparency throughout the process, including mechanisms for public reporting and accountability.

Conclusion

In conclusion, the amendment of the South African Constitution to allow land expropriation without compensation marks a decisive and necessary reform aimed at addressing the long-standing land inequalities deeply embedded in the country's historical trajectory. The current constitutional framework, particularly Section 25, was crafted to safeguard property rights, but in doing so, it has inadvertently stifled the potential for genuine and comprehensive land reform. While the intent of protecting property ownership is understandable, the requirement for compensation has created substantial obstacles, often resulting in delays, increased costs, and bureaucratic complexities that make the expropriation process inefficient. These challenges have severely undermined the government's ability to address the profound historical land dispossessions that continue to affect the lives of millions of South Africans, particularly the black majority.[154]

The enduring legacy of apartheid and colonialism manifests itself most starkly in the unequal distribution of land. Despite the end of institutionalised racial segregation, the ownership of land has remained disproportionately skewed in favour of the white minority, leaving the vast majority of black South Africans still marginalised from the country's most valuable resource. Efforts to redress these imbalances through the existing legal and constitutional mechanisms have proven inadequate, as the principle of compensation, while well-intentioned, has been weaponised to stall meaningful progress. This has not only prolonged the socio-economic exclusion of millions but also fuelled growing discontent, threatening the fragile peace and stability that South Africa has worked hard to build since the dawn of democracy.

The proposed amendment to the Constitution offers an opportunity to rectify this imbalance. By removing the requirement for compensation, the government would be empowered to take swift and decisive action in redistributing land to those who were historically dispossessed. This reform is not merely a symbolic gesture but a substantive change that could accelerate the process of land reform, making it more responsive to the urgent needs of the people. It would remove one of the key barriers that has hindered the effective implementation of land policies and enable a more direct approach to redistributing land in a way that addresses long-standing grievances.

Importantly, this proposed amendment is not without precedent, and South Africa can draw lessons from the experiences of other nations that have pursued similar policies. Countries like Zimbabwe and Venezuela offer cautionary tales of the challenges that can arise when such reforms are poorly implemented or lack sufficient legal and institutional support.

---

[154] Constitution of the Republic of South Africa, 1996, s 25.

However, South Africa has a unique opportunity to learn from these examples, adopting best practices while avoiding the pitfalls that have plagued other nations. A well-thought-out legal framework, coupled with strong governance and oversight, will be essential in ensuring that land expropriation without compensation is carried out in a manner that is both just and sustainable.

Critics of this amendment often raise concerns about its potential economic impact, arguing that it could deter investment and destabilise the agricultural sector. However, these concerns, while not entirely unfounded, must be weighed against the social and economic benefits that come with rectifying historical injustices. A more equitable distribution of land could, in fact, stimulate economic growth by enabling greater participation in the economy by previously marginalised groups. Moreover, it would foster social cohesion by addressing one of the most contentious and unresolved issues in post-apartheid South Africa—land ownership.

The proposed constitutional amendment to allow for land expropriation without compensation is a critical step towards achieving a more just and equitable society. It represents an opportunity to not only rectify the historical wrongs of dispossession but also to create a future where the wealth and resources of the country are more fairly shared among all its people. With a carefully crafted implementation strategy, grounded in the principles of justice, fairness, and sustainability, this reform has the potential to transform South Africa's socio-economic landscape, paving the way for a more inclusive and prosperous nation. The time has come for bold and decisive action, and the amendment of the Constitution is a necessary and transformative step towards realising the long-overdue promise of land justice in South Afric

6. VOICES FROM THE GROUND

The discourse surrounding land expropriation without compensation has largely been dominated by policymakers, legal experts, and economists, who often approach the topic through a lens of constitutional law, economic stability, and regulatory frameworks. These debates, while important, tend to centre around abstract principles and theoretical implications, sometimes losing sight of the very real human dimensions at the core of the issue. The intricacies of policy formulation and the legal challenges that accompany land expropriation are certainly critical to the broader conversation, but they only tell part of the story. The real essence of this issue lies in the lived realities of ordinary South Africans—individuals and communities whose lives have been profoundly shaped by the historical injustices of land dispossession, and who continue to live with the scars of these past wrongs.

This chapter seeks to centre these human stories, delving into the voices and experiences of those who have been directly impacted by land dispossession and who now find themselves at the forefront of the struggle for land restitution. It explores the daily realities of communities who have long been sidelined in the national conversation, bringing to light the deep frustrations, aspirations, and resilience of people who see land reclamation as essential to their dignity and identity. These are the voices of farmworkers, rural villagers, and urban dwellers alike, whose histories and futures are intricately tied to the land. For them, land expropriation without compensation is not merely a legal issue, but a crucial step towards righting the wrongs of the past and ensuring a more just and equitable future.

The chapter further examines the ongoing struggles faced by these communities as they navigate the challenges of land claims, often in the face of bureaucratic delays, legal obstacles, and sometimes hostile opposition. It highlights the grassroots movements and civil society organisations that have risen to advocate for these communities, playing a crucial role in amplifying their voices and pushing for meaningful change. Through these stories, the chapter paints a vivid picture of the human impact of land dispossession and the urgent need for a resolution that acknowledges and addresses the deep injustices that have been inflicted.

In doing so, this chapter aims to provide a more comprehensive understanding of land expropriation, one that goes beyond the legal and economic arguments to consider the profound social and emotional dimensions of the issue. It underscores that land is not just about territory or resources, but about history, memory, and the fundamental rights of individuals and communities to reclaim what was unjustly taken from them. Ultimately, this chapter argues that any discussion on land expropriation must start with these voices, for they are the true bearers of the land's legacy and the rightful claimants to its future.

Land as Identity and Ancestral Heritage

For many South Africans, the connection to the land is far more profound than the notions of ownership or economic survival often discussed in policy debates. It is a deep and enduring bond that forms the very foundation of their cultural, spiritual, and communal identity. The land is not merely a piece of property or a source of livelihood; it is considered a living entity, a provider of life and sustenance, and a guardian of ancestral heritage and traditions. This relationship between people and the land is steeped in reverence and respect, built over centuries through cultural practices, spiritual rituals, and oral histories that have been carefully passed down through generations.[155]

In many rural communities, the elders play a pivotal role in preserving and transmitting these traditions. They often recount stories of a time when their ancestors lived in close harmony with the land. These narratives are rich with detail, painting vivid pictures of a way of life that

---

[155] Sam Moyo and Kojo Sebastian Amanor, *Land and Sustainable Development in Africa* (Zed Books 2008).

was deeply connected to the natural world. The land was more than just a means of survival; it was an integral part of the community's identity and spirituality. The cycles of nature—the planting and harvesting of crops, the changing of seasons, the migrations of animals—were all understood and respected as part of a larger, interconnected system of life. The land was treated with care and reverence, as it was seen as the source of all sustenance and the repository of the community's collective memory and identity.

These stories are not just historical accounts; they are imbued with a deep sense of loss and longing for a time when the bond between the people and the land was unbroken. The forced removals and land seizures that occurred during colonialism and apartheid did more than just displace people from their homes—they severed this vital connection, leaving behind a legacy of trauma and dislocation that continues to affect communities to this day. The loss of land meant the loss of not only a physical space but also a cultural and spiritual anchor. The pain of this dislocation is palpable in the stories of those who lived through it, as well as in the lives of their descendants who inherit the legacy of dispossession.

For many, the land represents a link to their ancestors—a tangible connection to the past that holds the memories, struggles, and triumphs of those who came before them. The land is seen as a sacred space where the spirits of the ancestors reside, and where the living can commune with those who have passed on. It is a place where important life events—such as births, marriages, and funerals—are marked by rituals that honour the connection between the physical and spiritual worlds. This spiritual relationship with the land is a source of strength and resilience, providing communities with a sense of continuity and belonging, even in the face of adversity.[156]

The disconnection from the land has had profound and lasting effects on these communities. The trauma of being forcibly removed from their ancestral lands, of seeing their homes and livelihoods destroyed, has left deep scars. Many communities have struggled to maintain their cultural practices and traditions in the absence of the land that gave them

---

[156] Moyo and Amanor, *Land and Sustainable Development in Africa* (n157)

meaning. The sense of loss is not just about the physical land, but about the erosion of a way of life that was intimately tied to that land. This loss has been compounded by the ongoing marginalisation and economic hardships faced by those who were displaced, many of whom have been relegated to the peripheries of society, far from the land that once sustained them.

In this context, the call for land restitution and expropriation without compensation is not just about correcting economic imbalances or addressing historical injustices. It is about reclaiming a fundamental part of the community's identity and restoring the cultural and spiritual connection to the land that was severed by dispossession. For many, the return of the land is seen as essential to healing the wounds of the past and rebuilding the social fabric that was torn apart by the forces of colonialism and apartheid. It is about restoring dignity and autonomy to communities that have been disempowered and marginalised for generations.

The process of reclaiming the land is also seen as a way to revitalise and preserve cultural practices and traditions that have been endangered by displacement. By returning to the land, communities hope to revive the agricultural practices, rituals, and oral traditions that have been passed down through generations, ensuring that they are not lost to future generations. The land is seen as a living repository of cultural knowledge, a space where the wisdom of the ancestors can be accessed and where new generations can learn and grow in harmony with the natural world.

In this way, the struggle for land is not just a political or economic issue—it is a deeply personal and collective journey towards reclaiming identity, culture, and spiritual belonging. The land is seen as a source of empowerment, a foundation upon which communities can rebuild their lives and their futures. For many South Africans, the return of the land represents the possibility of healing, reconciliation, and a new beginning, where the wounds of the past can be addressed, and a more just and equitable society can be built.

In the rural areas of South Africa, the struggle for land is not merely a historical grievance but an ongoing and deeply embedded reality that continues to shape the lives and futures of countless individuals and communities. The issue of land access and ownership cuts to the core of their existence, affecting everything from their economic survival to their social cohesion and cultural identity. For small-scale farmers, agricultural labourers, and rural dwellers, land is much more than a piece of property—it is their lifeline, the foundation upon which their entire way of life is built. It is a source of sustenance, providing the food they grow and the means by which they earn their living. But it is also a symbol of autonomy, dignity, and belonging, representing their connection to their ancestors and their rightful place in the world.

Despite the many promises made by successive governments since the end of apartheid, the reality is that the distribution of land in South Africa remains starkly unequal. The vast majority of productive land is still controlled by a small, predominantly white minority, while the black majority, particularly in rural areas, continues to suffer the consequences of historical dispossession. This disparity is not just a statistic but a lived experience for millions of South Africans who wake up each day facing the harsh realities of landlessness. For these communities, the dream of land reform has yet to materialise in any meaningful way, leaving them trapped In a cycle of poverty, dependence, and frustration.

In many rural areas, land is the cornerstone of economic survival. It is the primary means through which communities sustain themselves, providing the resources necessary for growing crops, raising livestock, and building homes. Without access to sufficient and fertile land, many rural families are forced into precarious livelihoods, struggling to make ends meet on small plots that are often not enough to feed their families, let alone generate any significant income. The lack of access to land has also led to overcrowding in some rural areas, as multiple generations are forced to live on increasingly small and fragmented plots. This overcrowding exacerbates poverty and limits the opportunities for economic growth and development within these communities.[157]

The frustrations of these rural communities are palpable. For them, the promise of land reform was not just a political slogan but a hope for a better future—a future where they could reclaim their ancestral lands,

---

[157] Moyo and Amanor, *Land and Sustainable Development in Africa* (n157)

build sustainable livelihoods, and create a prosperous and equitable society for their children. However, the slow and often ineffective pace of land reform has left many feeling betrayed and disillusioned. Decades after the end of apartheid, they see little change in their circumstances, and the disparities in land ownership remain largely unchanged. The ongoing concentration of land in the hands of a few, coupled with the lack of meaningful support for small-scale farmers, has deepened the sense of injustice and inequality that pervades these communities.

In interviews and community meetings, rural dwellers express a deep sense of abandonment by the government and the broader society. They speak of the broken promises that have left them in a state of perpetual insecurity, unable to plan for the future or improve their living conditions. The daily struggles they face—such as limited access to water, poor soil quality, lack of infrastructure, and the challenges of climate change—are not just inconveniences but existential threats to their survival. Without adequate support and resources, many small-scale farmers are unable to make their land productive, leading to a vicious cycle where poverty begets more poverty.

For these communities, the debate over land expropriation without compensation is not an abstract or ideological discussion; it is a matter of immediate and pressing concern. They see it as the only viable solution to rectify the deep-seated inequalities that continue to define their lives. Land expropriation without compensation represents, for many, a long-overdue step towards justice—a way to address the historical wrongs of colonialism and apartheid and to create a more equitable distribution of land in the present. It is seen as a necessary corrective to a system that has failed them time and time again, leaving them with little hope of improving their circumstances without radical intervention.

The sense of urgency surrounding land reform In these rural areas cannot be overstated. For many, the stakes are nothing less than life or death. Without land, they cannot feed their families, build homes, or sustain their communities. The lack of land also means a lack of opportunity—a lack of the ability to break free from the cycle of poverty and dependence that has trapped so many rural South Africans for generations. The frustration and anger felt by these communities are driven by a deep sense of injustice, a belief that they have been denied not just their land but their right to a dignified life.

The ongoing struggle for land In rural South Africa is a powerful reminder of the unfinished business of the country's transition to democracy. While political freedom was achieved in 1994, economic and social justice remain elusive for many, particularly in rural areas where the legacy of dispossession continues to cast a long shadow. The voices of these communities make it clear that until the issue of land is resolved, the promise of a truly equitable and just South Africa will remain unfulfilled. For them, land expropriation without compensation is not just about righting historical wrongs but about securing a future where they can live with dignity, autonomy, and hope.

The Role of Women and Youth in Land Reform

Despite their importance, traditional governance systems face significant criticisms. One major concern is the lack of accountability and transparency in traditional land management. Decisions made by traditional leaders can sometimes lack clarity and public oversight, which may lead to perceptions of favouritism towards specific individuals or groups. This can erode trust in the traditional system and foster perceptions of nepotism or corruption.

Gender inequality is another significant issue within traditional systems, where women often face limitations on their land rights. Customary practices may restrict women's access to land, impacting their economic opportunities and perpetuating gender disparities. Additionally, younger community members might be excluded from decision-making processes, hindering their potential contributions to land management and development.

Moreover, the traditional governance system can reinforce existing power imbalances, as those in authority may wield disproportionate influence over land allocation and use. This can entrench social inequalities and hinder the equitable distribution of resources among community members.

Addressing these criticisms requires a nuanced approach. Enhancing transparency in land allocation and decision-making processes is vital to mitigate issues of accountability and ensure fair and open decision-making. Promoting inclusivity by involving marginalised groups, such as women and younger individuals, in land governance can help address gender and generational disparities.

Balancing traditional practices with modern legal frameworks is crucial. Integrating aspects of customary law with contemporary governance approaches can reconcile respect for cultural heritage with the need for equity and justice. Engaging communities in the design and implementation of land reforms ensures culturally sensitive changes that address specific needs and rights.

Educational initiatives and capacity building for traditional leaders and community members can enhance understanding of land rights and governance practices, fostering more equitable land management. Establishing mechanisms for monitoring and evaluating land reform efforts is essential to track progress, identify challenges, and adjust strategies for sustainable and just outcomes. Through a combination of transparency, inclusivity, balance, education, and rigorous evaluation, it is possible to address the complexities of traditional land management while advancing fair and equitable land reform.

Women, especially in rural areas, are the heartbeat of agriculture and the guardians of family land in South Africa. Their role extends far beyond the physical labour they perform in the fields; it is intertwined with the very fabric of rural life and the survival of their communities. From dawn until dusk, these women are engaged in the arduous tasks of tilling the soil, planting seeds, nurturing crops, and harvesting the produce that feeds their families and often entire communities. Their work is both relentless and indispensable, ensuring that their households have food on the table and that the local economy remains viable.[158]

However, despite their central role in agriculture and land management, women face significant and persistent barriers when it

---

[158] R S Strickland, *To Have and to Hold: Women's Property and Inheritance Rights in the Context of HIV/AIDS in Sub-Saharan Africa* (Working Paper, International Center for Research on Women 2004).

comes to owning and controlling the land they work on. These barriers are rooted in deeply entrenched patriarchal structures that have, for generations, dictated the social, economic, and legal frameworks within which land ownership is determined. In many rural communities, the transfer of land ownership is governed by customs and laws that favour male heirs, effectively excluding women from land ownership or relegating them to a secondary status. This gendered disparity is not just a matter of tradition but has profound implications for the lives of women, their families, and their communities.

The patriarchal norms that dictate land ownership are often reinforced by broader societal structures, including legal systems that fail to adequately protect women's rights to land. In many cases, even when women have some form of legal claim to the land, these rights are insecure and can be easily overridden by male relatives or community leaders who wield greater power and influence. For instance, in the event of a husband's death, a widow may find her rights to the family land challenged by male relatives, leaving her vulnerable and without a secure means to support her children. This precariousness is exacerbated by the fact that women are often excluded from decision-making processes at both the community and household levels, further limiting their ability to assert their rights and protect their interests.

The consequences of this systemic exclusion are far-reaching. Women who are denied secure land rights are often forced into a position of economic dependency on male relatives, which in turn perpetuates cycles of poverty and inequality. Without the ability to own and control land, women are unable to make long-term investments in the land's productivity, such as improving soil quality, building irrigation systems, or planting perennial crops that could provide sustainable income. This lack of investment not only limits their economic opportunities but also undermines the overall productivity and resilience of the agricultural sector in these communities.

Moreover, the lack of secure land rights leaves women vulnerable to various forms of exploitation and abuse. In some cases, women may be coerced into unfavourable agreements or forced to give up their land rights in exchange for short-term support or protection from male relatives or community leaders. This vulnerability is compounded by the fact that women often lack access to legal resources and education, making it difficult for them to challenge these exploitative practices or to seek redress through formal legal channels.[159]

Despite these formidable challenges, the voices of women in rural South African communities are filled with a remarkable sense of determination and resilience. They speak passionately about their desire for secure land rights, not just for themselves but for their children and future generations. They understand that having secure ownership of the land they cultivate would allow them to plan for the future, invest in the land's productivity, and provide a stable and sustainable livelihood for their families. For these women, land ownership is not just about economic survival; it is about autonomy, dignity, and the ability to shape their own destinies.

Many women see the ongoing debate around land expropriation without compensation as a potential turning point—a moment of opportunity where the historical injustices of land dispossession could finally be addressed, and where the deeply entrenched gender inequalities that have long denied them equal access to land could be dismantled. They hope that this process will lead to a more equitable distribution of land, one that recognises and respects the rights of women as equal stakeholders and contributors to their communities' well-being.

However, alongside this hope, there is a palpable concern that without specific provisions to safeguard women's rights, land reform efforts could inadvertently reinforce existing inequalities. Women fear that if land expropriation and redistribution are carried out without a conscious focus on gender equity, they could once again be marginalised in the process, with land being allocated primarily to men or to those with greater social and economic power. This concern is not unfounded, given the historical patterns of exclusion and marginalisation that have characterised land ownership in South Africa and many other parts of

---

[159] R S Strickland, *To Have and to Hold: Women's Property and Inheritance Rights in the Context of HIV/AIDS in Sub-Saharan Africa* (Working Paper, International Center for Research on Women 2004).

the world.

To prevent this outcome, it is crucial that any land reform initiatives, including land expropriation without compensation, are designed and implemented with a strong emphasis on gender equality. This means not only ensuring that women are explicitly included in the distribution of land but also that they are provided with the necessary legal, financial, and educational support to secure and defend their rights. Legal reforms that recognise and protect women's land rights are essential, as are educational programmes that inform women of their rights and how to exercise them. Additionally, efforts to challenge and change the patriarchal norms that restrict women's access to land must be an integral part of the land reform process.

Supporting women in agriculture should also extend beyond just land ownership. It should involve providing them with access to resources such as credit, seeds, tools, and training, which are essential for making the land productive and ensuring long-term agricultural sustainability. By equipping women with these resources, land reform can help to transform not only the lives of individual women but also the broader rural economies in which they live and work.

Moreover, the recognition and support of women's roles in agriculture and land management should be accompanied by efforts to elevate their voices in decision-making processes. Women's perspectives and experiences are invaluable in shaping policies and practices that promote sustainable and equitable land use. Ensuring that women have a seat at the table—both in local community governance and in broader national policy discussions—is crucial for the success of any land reform initiative.

The ongoing struggle for land rights among women in rural South Africa is a testament to their resilience, strength, and unwavering commitment to justice. Their fight for secure land ownership is not just about correcting the wrongs of the past; it is about building a future where women are recognised as equal partners in the stewardship of the land and the creation of a more just and equitable society. Land reform, if done right, holds the potential to empower these women, to lift them out of poverty, and to enable them to contribute more fully to the economic and social development of their communities.

In this context, land reform is not just a policy issue; it is a moral imperative. It is about recognising the invaluable contributions of women to agriculture and community life, and about ensuring that they have the rights and resources they need to thrive. As South Africa continues to grapple with the complex legacy of land dispossession, the voices of women in rural areas must be heard, their rights must be protected, and their contributions must be valued. Only then can the promise of land reform be fully realised, creating a more just and equitable future for all.

South Africa's youth, who comprise a substantial portion of the population, view land reform as a critical issue that could shape their future. In a country where unemployment rates among young people are alarmingly high, many young South Africans see access to land as a crucial pathway to securing a livelihood, fostering economic independence, and building a stable future for themselves and their families. This perspective is particularly prevalent in rural areas, where traditional means of income are dwindling, and opportunities for young people are scarce. The land, with its potential to provide sustenance, economic opportunity, and a sense of belonging, is seen as a beacon of hope In an otherwise challenging economic landscape.

However, despite this optimism, there is a deep-seated sense of disillusionment among many young people. The slow pace of land reform and the bureaucratic hurdles that have hindered progress have left them feeling disconnected from the process. For years, they have witnessed their parents and grandparents struggle to secure land, often battling against a system that seems more focused on maintaining the status quo than on addressing the inequalities that continue to plague rural communities. This generational struggle has fostered a growing cynicism among the youth, who worry that they too will be denied the opportunity to build a life on the land—a life that should be their birthright.

The frustration felt by young people is palpable. They see the lack of access to land not just as an economic barrier, but as a symbol of broader social and political exclusion. Many have grown up in communities where the promises of land reform have been slow to materialise, and where opportunities for economic advancement are limited to those with the means to navigate a complex and often opaque system. For these young people, land expropriation without compensation is not just a policy issue; it is a matter of justice and survival. It represents a chance to break free from the cycle of poverty and marginalisation that has defined their lives and the lives of their ancestors.

Despite these challenges, the voices of the youth are also filled with hope, resilience, and an unwavering determination to change their circumstances. They speak passionately about their dreams of starting businesses, creating jobs, and developing their communities. Many have innovative ideas for how to use the land to create sustainable livelihoods, from launching agricultural enterprises that could feed their communities and generate income, to developing eco-tourism projects that could attract visitors and stimulate local economies. These young people are not simply looking for handouts; they are seeking the opportunity to contribute meaningfully to their society, to be the drivers of economic growth and social change.

However, the realisation of these dreams is contingent on more than just access to land. The youth recognise that they need support in terms of training, resources, and infrastructure to turn their ideas into reality. They call for practical skills training in agriculture, entrepreneurship, and sustainable land management, as well as access to financial resources such as credit and grants to help them get their projects off the ground. Additionally, they highlight the need for improved infrastructure—such as roads, water supply, and electricity—that would enable them to fully utilise the land and connect their products to broader markets.

For South Africa's youth, land reform is about more than rectifying the injustices of the past; it is about building a future where they can thrive. It is about creating a society where young people have the opportunity to realise their potential, to become leaders and innovators, and to contribute to the prosperity and stability of their nation. In this sense, land reform is not just an economic imperative, but a social and moral one as well. It is about empowering a generation to take control of their destinies and to build a future that is more just, equitable, and sustainable for all South Africans.

The determination of the youth to be active participants in land reform underscores the urgency of addressing their needs and aspirations. Their energy and creativity, if harnessed and supported, could drive a new wave of development in rural areas, transforming underutilised land into vibrant centres of economic activity. However, without the necessary support, there is a risk that their potential will be wasted, and their frustrations will continue to grow.

South Africa's youth view land reform as a crucial issue that directly impacts their future prospects. They are eager to break the cycle of poverty and marginalisation that has affected their families for generations and are determined to use land as a means of creating sustainable livelihoods. However, to achieve this, they need more than just access to land; they require the training, resources, and infrastructure that will enable them to succeed. As the country continues to grapple with the complexities of land reform, it is essential that the voices of the youth are heard and that their needs are met, ensuring that they can play a leading role in shaping the future of South Africa.

The Urban Land Crisis in South Africa

In South Africa's rapidly expanding urban areas, the struggle for land has intensified, largely driven by the overwhelming demand for affordable housing and basic infrastructure. As cities grow, the gap between land supply and demand has widened, exacerbating a housing crisis that affects millions of people. Many South Africans are forced to live in informal settlements and townships, where overcrowding and inadequate living conditions are widespread. These areas often lack essential services such as clean water, sanitation, and electricity, creating significant challenges for residents. The escalating cost of land and housing in urban centres has further compounded these issues, making it increasingly difficult for low-income families to secure affordable and stable housing. This situation has led to a deepening crisis that disproportionately impacts the most vulnerable populations.

The sense of frustration among urban residents is profound. Many feel that the promises of the post-apartheid era have not been fulfilled, leaving them in a state of disenchantment as they struggle with daily hardships. Informal settlements are frequently plagued by the threat of evictions and demolitions, with residents living under constant fear of losing their homes. Additionally, these communities often face high levels of violence and crime, which further exacerbates their sense of insecurity. In this context, land expropriation without compensation is perceived by many as a critical tool for addressing the housing crisis and ensuring that all South Africans have access to safe and affordable housing. It is seen as a necessary measure to rectify historical inequalities and provide a more secure living environment for those who have been marginalised.

Urban land reform also needs to address broader issues related to spatial justice and the lingering impacts of apartheid-era planning. The legacy of apartheid has left many black South Africans living in areas that are physically distant from economic opportunities and essential services. This historical segregation has perpetuated spatial inequalities, with marginalised communities often cut off from the economic benefits of urban growth. As cities expand, there is an urgent need to address these spatial disparities and create more Inclusive and equitable urban environments.

Residents from these urban communities call for a reimagining of city planning that goes beyond merely addressing the shortage of affordable housing. They advocate for a vision of urban development that incorporates broader aspects of spatial justice, ensuring equitable access to green spaces, public transportation, and economic opportunities. Such a vision would involve creating well-planned urban areas where all residents have the chance to thrive. This includes not only improving housing conditions but also integrating essential services and infrastructure into urban planning to support sustainable and equitable growth.

To achieve this vision, urban land reform must be comprehensive and inclusive. It requires not only the redistribution of land but also substantial investment in infrastructure and services that support equitable development. Addressing the immediate need for affordable housing is crucial, but it must be accompanied by efforts to improve living conditions in informal settlements and underserved areas. Investments in essential services such as water, sanitation, and electricity are necessary to enhance the quality of life for residents. Additionally, improving public transportation systems can help connect marginalised areas with economic hubs, enabling residents to access job opportunities and essential services.

Economic development within these communities is also essential. Supporting local businesses, fostering entrepreneurship, and providing job training and skills development programmes can create opportunities for economic advancement and help break the cycle of poverty. Access to green spaces and recreational areas is important for enhancing the overall quality of life and environmental sustainability. Ensuring that urban planning processes are participatory and inclusive allows residents to have a say in decisions that affect their lives, leading to more effective and responsive solutions.

The struggle for land in South Africa's urban areas is marked by severe housing shortages, spatial injustice, and the enduring impacts of apartheid-era planning. Land expropriation without compensation is seen as a critical tool for addressing these challenges and providing equitable access to housing. However, a comprehensive approach to urban land reform must also address broader issues of spatial justice and infrastructure development. By reimagining urban spaces and investing in necessary resources and services, it is possible to create more inclusive, vibrant cities where all residents have the opportunity to improve their lives and contribute to a more equitable society.

The role of traditional leaders in land reform is multifaceted and deeply intertwined with the cultural and social dynamics of rural communities. Traditional leaders, often known as amakhosi, play a crucial role in various governance functions related to land management under customary law. They are responsible for allocating land to community members according to traditional norms, mediating disputes over land use and ownership, and safeguarding cultural practices linked to the land. By performing these roles, they help maintain community cohesion and uphold historical land use practices.

The voices from the ground provide a powerful and often overlooked perspective on the land reform debate. These voices, rooted in the lived experiences of South Africans from all walks of life, reveal the deep and multifaceted nature of the land issue. They remind us that land reform is not just about legal frameworks and economic policies but about justice, dignity, and the fulfillment of a long-held aspiration for a better future.

As the struggle for land reform continues, it is crucial that these voices are not just heard but are actively included in shaping the policies and strategies that will determine the future of land in South Africa. The people whose lives are most affected by land reform must be empowered to participate in the decision-making process, ensuring that their needs, aspirations, and rights are fully taken into account.

Incorporating these voices into the broader debate means acknowledging the complexities of the land issue, which varies across different communities. It requires a commitment to a people-centred approach to land reform, one that goes beyond the rhetoric of policy and addresses the real, everyday challenges that people face. This approach must be grounded in the recognition that land is more than just an economic asset; it is a source of identity, culture, and social stability.

The power of the people's voice lies In its ability to bring to light the human dimensions of land reform. These voices challenge us to think critically about the kind of society we want to build and the values that will guide our actions. They remind us that land reform is not an abstract policy issue but a matter of justice and human dignity.

As South Africa moves forward with land expropriation without compensation, it is essential to keep these voices at the forefront of the discussion. The success of land reform will ultimately be judged by its ability to improve the lives of ordinary South Africans, to restore their connection to the land, and to create a more just and equitable society.

Conclusion

In conclusion, the voices from the ground are not merely participants in the ongoing land reform debate—they are, in fact, the driving force behind it. These voices are the heart of the movement, representing the lived realities of those who have historically been marginalised and dispossessed. They speak from a place of deep connection to the land, a connection that is not merely economic but also cultural, social, and spiritual. These voices encapsulate the hopes, dreams, and determination of communities who seek not just to reclaim land, but to reclaim their dignity, identity, and future.

The experiences, struggles, and aspirations of these communities must be the cornerstone of the land reform process. Every step, from the drafting of legislation to the detailed implementation of policies, must be informed by their insights. It is not enough for policymakers and legislators to consider these voices as one of many factors; they must be central to the decision-making process. This means creating spaces where these voices are actively listened to, where their concerns are addressed, and where their knowledge is valued. It requires a shift In perspective—from seeing these communities as passive beneficiaries of land reform to recognising them as active agents of change who hold the key to the success of the entire endeavour.

Moreover, empowering these voices means more than just consulting them; it means giving them real power and agency in shaping the outcomes of land reform. This involves not only participatory processes but also ensuring that the resources, support, and mechanisms are in place for these communities to effectively contribute to and benefit from land reform. The goal should be to create a land reform process that is truly inclusive, one that acknowledges and addresses the historical injustices faced by these communities while also paving the way for sustainable and equitable development.

By prioritising and empowering these voices, South Africa can ensure that land reform becomes more than just a policy exercise or a response to political pressures. It can become a transformative process that addresses the root causes of inequality and social discontent. A land reform process that is deeply rooted in the experiences and aspirations of those most affected can lead to the redistribution of land in a manner that fosters social justice, economic empowerment, and community resilience.

It can help to rebuild trust between the state and its citizens, create opportunities for economic growth that benefit the many rather than the few, and contribute to a more cohesive and united society.

Ultimately, the success of land reform hinges on its ability to be truly transformative. This can only be achieved if the process is driven by those whose lives and futures are most intertwined with the land. By listening to and empowering these voices, South Africa can create a land reform process that not only rectifies the injustices of the past but also lays the foundation for a more just and prosperous future for all. The voices from the ground are not just participants in the land reform debate—they are its driving force, and their centrality to the process is the key to unlocking a future where land reform serves the people and contributes to the creation of a society that is fair, inclusive, and prosperous.

7. THE CASE FOR REGIME CHANGE

Land expropriation remains one of South Africa's most contentious and pivotal issues, central to the ongoing discourse about equity and economic justice. The effectiveness of land reform policies has been a major point of debate, particularly given the long-standing governance of the African National Congress (ANC). While the ANC has implemented various land reform initiatives over the years, the debate has intensified over whether these measures have been effective in addressing historical injustices and achieving meaningful land redistribution.

The ANC's approach to land reform has been marked by a combination of policy frameworks, including the Promotion of National Unity and Reconciliation Act, the Land Reform (Labour Tenants) Act, and the Restitution of Land Rights Act. However, despite these efforts, there are significant criticisms regarding the speed, effectiveness, and equity of the land reform process. Critics argue that the ANC's policies have often been hampered by bureaucratic inefficiencies, lack of political will, and inadequate support for beneficiaries. Additionally, there have been concerns about the slow pace of land redistribution and the persistence of land ownership inequalities.[160]

Given these challenges, this chapter argues that regime change is not only beneficial but crucial for the successful implementation of land expropriation. A new political leadership could bring fresh perspectives and approaches to land reform, potentially overcoming the limitations of the ANC's current strategies. The potential advantages of new political leadership in this context include increased accountability, innovative

---

[160] Sam Moyo and Kojo Sebastian Amanor, *Land and Sustainable Development in Africa* (Zed Books 2008).

policy solutions, and a renewed focus on the needs of marginalised communities.

Steve Biko's assertion that "The most potent weapon in the hands of the oppressor is the mind of the oppressed"[161] highlights the importance of shifting perspectives and breaking free from outdated approaches. A change in regime could address some of the key criticisms of the ANC's land reform approach. For instance, new leadership might prioritise more effective and transparent implementation of land reform policies, ensuring that resources are allocated efficiently and that beneficiaries receive the necessary support to make the most of their land. Additionally, a different political leadership could be more responsive to the evolving needs of the population, adapting land reform strategies to address contemporary challenges and opportunities.

Furthermore, new political leadership could potentially bring greater political will and commitment to addressing land reform issues. The urgency of land redistribution and the need to rectify historical injustices require a proactive and determined approach. A regime change might inject new energy into the land reform process, leading to more decisive action and innovative solutions that could accelerate progress and achieve transformative outcomes.

It is also worth noting that regime change could foster a more inclusive and participatory approach to land reform. New political leadership might be more inclined to engage with a broader range of stakeholders, including civil society organisations, community groups, and experts, to ensure that land reform policies are developed and implemented in a way that genuinely addresses the needs and concerns of affected communities. This inclusive approach could help build greater consensus and support for land reform initiatives, enhancing their effectiveness and sustainability.

Moreover, the potential for regime change could stimulate a more rigorous evaluation of existing land reform policies and practices. New leadership might conduct comprehensive reviews of past initiatives, identifying successes and shortcomings, and using these insights to inform future strategies. This evidence-based approach could lead to

---

[161] S Biko, *I Write What I Like* (Picador Africa 2002).

more effective and targeted land reform policies that better achieve the goals of equitable land distribution and economic empowerment.

Regime Change and Radical Land Reform

A change in political leadership could offer a valuable opportunity to overcome the limitations of current strategies and implement more effective land reform measures. By bringing fresh perspectives, increased political will, and a more inclusive approach, new leadership could play a crucial role in achieving transformative land reform and addressing the historical injustices that have long plagued South African society.

Under the ANC's rule, land reform has been characterised by a cautious and incremental approach rather than bold, transformative action. This strategy has involved making numerous compromises with commercial farmers and landowners, resulting in market-driven solutions that have often fallen short of addressing the deep-seated inequalities in land ownership.

The ANC's land reform policies have included initiatives such as land restitution, land redistribution, and tenure reform. Land restitution aims to return land to individuals or communities dispossessed under apartheid, while land redistribution seeks to transfer land from historically privileged owners to previously disadvantaged groups. Tenure reform focuses on securing land rights for those occupying land but lacking formal ownership. Despite these efforts, the pace of reform has been slow, and the implementation has faced significant challenges.

Critics argue that the ANC's approach has been overly accommodating to existing landowners and commercial interests, which has diluted the impact of the reform measures. The reliance on market-driven solutions has led to protracted negotiations and compromises that often favour the interests of current landholders over those of marginalised communities. As a result, the reform process has been marked by bureaucratic inefficiencies and delays, which have impeded progress and limited the benefits to the majority of landless and disadvantaged individuals.

The slow pace of land reform under the ANC has been attributed to several factors. These include the complex legal and administrative procedures involved in land transactions, resistance from vested interests, and the lack of sufficient resources and political will to drive the reform process forward. The ANC's approach has also been criticised for its lack of urgency and decisiveness, with many arguing that it has failed to address the root causes of land inequality and has not delivered on its promise of substantial and equitable land redistribution.

Furthermore, the compromises made with commercial farmers and landowners have led to a piecemeal and often inadequate redistribution of land. In some cases, the land transferred under the reform initiatives has been poorly managed or left fallow, failing to achieve the intended economic and social benefits. The resulting inefficiencies have exacerbated the disparity between landowners and the landless, leaving many South Africans still waiting for justice and equitable access to land.

The shortcomings of the ANC's land reform approach have led to growing disillusionment among many communities who continue to face the challenges of landlessness and marginalisation. The slow progress and the perceived inadequacies of the reform measures have heightened calls for a more effective and transformative approach to land redistribution, one that prioritises the needs of the disadvantaged and addresses the historical injustices that have long plagued South Africa's land ownership landscape.

Regime change presents a crucial opportunity to overcome the limitations of the ANC's approach and achieve meaningful land reform. New political leadership could bring fresh perspectives and a stronger commitment to addressing land inequalities. Parties such as the Economic Freedom Fighters (EFF) and the newly formed Mk (Umkhonto we Sizwe) Party advocate for more radical measures that could provide more direct and effective solutions to the problem of land ownership.

The EFF, under the leadership of Julius Malema, has championed the cause of expropriating land without compensation as a central policy. The party's stance is rooted in a desire to address historical injustices and redistribute wealth more equitably. The EFF argues that the current incremental approach has failed to adequately resolve the deep-seated inequalities in land ownership and that a more assertive policy is necessary to achieve meaningful change. By removing the compensation requirement, the EFF aims to expedite the redistribution process and ensure that land is transferred swiftly to those who have been historically disadvantaged.

Similarly, the new MK Party, which has emerged from the legacy of the Umkhonto we Sizwe (MK), the military wing of the ANC during the struggle against apartheid, advocates for a more assertive approach to land reform. The MK Party's platform focuses on addressing the economic and social imbalances created by apartheid and aims to implement land reform policies that reflect the radical principles of the liberation struggle. This includes prioritising land expropriation and seeking to rectify the disparities that have persisted despite years of reform efforts.

A regime change that brings these more radical parties into leadership could enable the adoption of bold policies that go beyond the incremental adjustments of the ANC. New leadership, unburdened by past compromises and entrenched interests, could pursue a more aggressive land reform agenda. This might involve implementing comprehensive strategies to tackle systemic land inequalities and ensuring that the benefits of reform reach those most in need. Such a shift could accelerate progress and deliver on the promises of land reform in ways that the current administration has struggled to achieve.

The EFF's and MK Party's approaches highlight the need for a transformative shift in land reform policies. The ANC's cautious approach and compromises with commercial farmers have often resulted in limited progress, leaving many landless and marginalised communities without the means to fully benefit from land reform. In contrast, a new political regime could implement reforms with greater urgency and resolve, addressing the root causes of land inequality and delivering tangible benefits to disadvantaged groups.

Moreover, a regime change could foster greater political will and public support for more transformative land reform policies. By engaging with a broad coalition of stakeholders and demonstrating a commitment to addressing land injustices, new leadership could build a stronger consensus for reform. This could lead to more effective implementation and a greater likelihood of achieving long-term success in redistributing land and promoting economic equity.

The prospect of regime change offers a significant opportunity to address the shortcomings of the ANC's land reform approach. New political leadership, such as that proposed by the EFF and the MK Party, could introduce more radical and effective measures, including the expropriation of land without compensation, to tackle land inequalities head-on. By adopting bold policies and demonstrating a stronger commitment to reform, a new regime could accelerate progress and achieve meaningful outcomes in land redistribution, addressing the historical injustices that have long hindered South Africa's path to equitable land ownership.

The ANC's reluctance to address the land question decisively is partly driven by a fear of antagonising white South Africans and the economic interests they represent. This hesitancy is exemplified by the ANC's recent coalition with the Democratic Alliance (DA) following the 2024 general and provincial elections. The DA, often perceived as representing predominantly white and conservative interests, has been criticised for its stance on land reform and race relations.

The coalition, presented as a "Government of National Unity," appears to be a strategic move aimed at maintaining political stability and appeasing various factions, rather than a genuine commitment to transformative land policies. This alliance underscores the ANC's cautious approach and its attempt to balance competing interests, which may be a reflection of its fear of confronting deeply entrenched land issues. The decision to form such a coalition suggests a reluctance to pursue radical land reform measures that could disrupt existing power dynamics and provoke strong reactions from influential economic stakeholders.

The ANC's approach to land reform has often been characterised by Incremental changes and compromises, influenced by the need to maintain political alliances and manage the potential backlash from powerful economic interests. This cautious stance has resulted in limited progress in addressing the systemic inequalities in land ownership and has left many disadvantaged communities waiting for the promised benefits of land reform.

By forming a coalition with the DA, the ANC has further complicated its ability to implement bold and transformative land policies. The DA's traditional stance on land reform, which tends to favour market-driven solutions and property rights, contrasts sharply with the more radical proposals advocated by parties like the Economic Freedom Fighters (EFF). This coalition reflects a broader strategic approach to governance that prioritises political stability and coalition management over addressing the urgent and often contentious issues related to land redistribution.

The ANC's fear of antagonising powerful economic interests and disrupting the status quo has thus contributed to its hesitant approach to land reform. The current coalition dynamics and political considerations may lead to continued incrementalism in land policy, leaving the deeper structural issues of land ownership unaddressed. This cautious approach may undermine efforts to achieve significant and equitable land redistribution, perpetuating existing inequalities and failing to deliver on the transformative potential of land reform.

The Potential Impact of New Political Leadership on Land Expropriation Efforts

New political leadership could offer significant advantages for land expropriation efforts. Fresh leadership might be more willing to implement bold and comprehensive land reform measures without being constrained by previous compromises or vested interests. This willingness to take decisive action could result in the introduction of policies that address the root causes of land inequality more effectively. Unlike current leaders who may be tied to existing power structures, new leaders could push through substantial changes and drive reforms with greater urgency and commitment.

Additionally, a new regime could provide a clear and coherent vision for land reform. This clarity would ensure that policies are not only focused but also effectively implemented. New leadership could bring a unified approach to the reform process, streamlining efforts and reducing bureaucratic obstacles that have previously hampered progress. With a well-defined strategy, new leaders could make significant strides in land redistribution, ensuring that efforts are targeted and impactful.

Increased accountability and transparency are other potential benefits of a regime change. New leaders may be more proactive in addressing the inefficiencies and corruption that have plagued current land reform initiatives. By fostering a greater sense of accountability, they could restore public trust in the land reform process. This would ensure that resources are used efficiently and that the benefits of reform are equitably distributed to those who need them most. Improved oversight could help to eliminate practices that have undermined previous efforts and enhance the overall effectiveness of land redistribution.

Furthermore, a change in political leadership could galvanise public and political support for land reform. New leaders might engage more effectively with various stakeholders, building broader coalitions and generating momentum for comprehensive reform. This increased support would create a more favourable environment for implementing transformative policies, allowing for a more robust and collaborative approach to addressing land issues. Enhanced public and political backing could facilitate the development of policies that not only address historical injustices but also advance social and economic equity.

Overall, the potential for new political leadership to offer decisive action, clear vision, increased accountability, and enhanced support highlights the opportunities that regime change could bring to land expropriation efforts. By overcoming the limitations of current approaches and addressing the systemic issues of land inequality, new leadership could drive meaningful reform and achieve significant progress in land redistribution.

While regime change holds promise for advancing land expropriation efforts, it is important to address potential challenges that may arise during political transitions. Such changes can create uncertainty, which may impact investor confidence and economic stability. This period of uncertainty could lead to fluctuations in investment flows and disruptions in economic activities, potentially complicating efforts to implement effective land reform.

New leadership must be prepared to navigate the complexities associated with land reform. This includes making necessary legal adjustments, engaging in negotiations with entrenched landowners, and managing the expectations of various stakeholders. The process of reform requires careful planning and strategic implementation to mitigate risks and ensure that the transition does not exacerbate existing challenges.

Ensuring that reforms are carried out transparently and fairly is crucial for maintaining stability and achieving lasting results. Transparent processes can build trust among stakeholders and reduce resistance to change. By clearly communicating the objectives and benefits of land reform, new leadership can foster greater understanding and support for the policies being implemented. Fairness in the execution of reforms will be vital to addressing historical grievances and achieving equitable outcomes, thereby enhancing the legitimacy and effectiveness of the reform efforts.

Overall, while regime change presents significant opportunities for advancing land expropriation, it must be approached with careful consideration of the associated challenges. By strategically managing the transition and prioritising transparency and fairness, new leadership can successfully implement land reform and achieve meaningful progress in addressing land inequalities.

If regime change leads to a more decisive approach to land expropriation, several positive outcomes could emerge. A more assertive and comprehensive land reform strategy could result in significant improvements in land distribution, addressing long-standing inequalities and providing previously marginalised communities with the opportunity to access and utilise land more effectively. This redistribution could foster economic empowerment among these communities, allowing them to engage in productive activities and build sustainable livelihoods.

Enhanced economic empowerment for previously marginalised groups could contribute to a reduction in socio-economic inequalities.

By giving disadvantaged communities access to land, new leadership could promote economic inclusion and support the development of local businesses and agricultural ventures. This shift could lead to more equitable wealth distribution and improved living standards for many.

Effective land reform could also have a positive impact on agricultural productivity. With better access to land, smallholder farmers could adopt modern farming practices, increase their crop yields, and contribute to greater national food security. Improved agricultural output would not only benefit local economies but also stimulate rural development through the creation of jobs and infrastructure improvements.

Moreover, a decisive approach to land reform could contribute to broader national economic growth. By addressing land ownership disparities and fostering agricultural productivity, new leadership could stimulate economic activity and attract investment. This, in turn, could support overall economic development and enhance the country's economic stability.

Conversely, poorly managed reforms or political instability resulting from regime change could undermine these potential benefits. Inadequate planning, lack of transparency, or ineffective implementation of land reform policies could lead to continued inequalities and failed expectations. Political instability could disrupt the reform process and create an environment of uncertainty, affecting investor confidence and economic stability.

It is crucial for any new leadership to approach land reform with a clear strategy and unwavering commitment to transparency and effectiveness. A well-organised and transparent approach will help to build trust among stakeholders, facilitate smooth implementation, and maximise the benefits of land expropriation. By addressing potential risks and ensuring that reforms are carried out fairly and efficiently, new leadership can harness the transformative potential of land expropriation to achieve meaningful and sustainable outcomes.

Conclusion

In conclusion, the case for regime change to effect land expropriation is both compelling and timely. While the ANC's incremental approach has made some progress in addressing land issues, it has not sufficiently tackled the deep-rooted and systemic problems of land inequality that continue to affect South Africa. The ANC's cautious and market-driven strategies, characterised by compromises with existing landowners and incremental adjustments, have not provided the bold and transformative solutions needed to rectify longstanding injustices in land distribution.

The limitations of the current approach are evident In the slow pace of reform and the persistent inequalities that remain. Despite various initiatives aimed at land restitution and redistribution, many South Africans, particularly those from previously marginalised communities, still face significant barriers to accessing land and benefiting from its economic potential. The incremental nature of these reforms has often resulted in half-measures that fail to address the scale of the problem comprehensively.

A new political regime could offer a fresh perspective and a more decisive approach to land expropriation. With new leadership, there is an opportunity to pursue more assertive and transformative policies that go beyond the cautious steps taken by the current administration. This regime change could bring about a clear and coherent vision for land reform, enabling the implementation of bold measures designed to address historical injustices and achieve meaningful land redistribution.

By embracing regime change, South Africa can seize the chance to overhaul its land reform strategy and address the deep-seated inequalities that have persisted for decades. A new political leadership could introduce policies that directly tackle the root causes of land inequality, ensuring that land expropriation is executed in a manner that is both fair and effective. This shift could revitalise the land reform process, making it more dynamic and responsive to the needs of those who have been historically disadvantaged.

Moreover, a decisive approach to land expropriation could contribute to broader socio-economic benefits. Effective land redistribution has the potential to enhance economic empowerment among previously marginalised communities, stimulate agricultural productivity, and drive rural development. By addressing land ownership disparities, new leadership could foster a more equitable society, reduce socio-economic inequalities, and support national economic growth.

The prospect of regime change represents a critical opportunity for advancing land expropriation efforts in South Africa. While the ANC's incremental approach has made some strides, it has not delivered the transformative outcomes needed to address deep-seated land inequalities. A new political regime could provide the decisive action, clear vision, and commitment necessary to implement comprehensive land reform, rectify historical injustices, and build a more equitable and prosperous future for all South Africans.

8. THE ECONOMIC BENEFITS OF LAND EXPROPRIATION

Land expropriation without compensation is more than just a policy; it is an economic imperative for South Africa. The history of land dispossession in this country has created deep-rooted economic inequalities that continue to define the socio-economic landscape today. From the colonial era to the apartheid regime, vast tracts of land were systematically taken from black South Africans, resulting in the concentration of land ownership in the hands of a privileged minority. This historical injustice has had far-reaching consequences, not only in terms of material deprivation but also in the erosion of cultural and social identity tied to the land.

The dispossession of land was not just a loss of physical space but also a denial of economic opportunities and autonomy. Land is a fundamental asset that underpins economic development, and its unequal distribution has entrenched poverty, limited access to economic resources, and stifled the potential for wealth creation among the dispossessed. The resulting imbalance has perpetuated cycles of poverty, unemployment, and economic exclusion, particularly in rural areas where land is central to livelihoods.

Moreover, the lack of access to land has had a cascading effect on housing, food security, and the ability to generate sustainable livelihoods. Urbanisation has intensified these challenges, as land scarcity and inflated property prices have forced many into informal settlements, further entrenching inequality. Without addressing the land question, efforts to tackle unemployment and poverty will remain inadequate, as land remains a cornerstone of economic empowerment and social justice.

In this context, land reform, particularly expropriation without compensation, is not just about rectifying historical wrongs; it is an urgent necessity to rebalance the scales of economic power and provide a foundation for a more equitable society. It is a step towards dismantling the structural inequalities that continue to marginalise the majority and an essential component of building a just and inclusive economy where all South Africans have the opportunity to thrive.

Land expropriation, when executed thoughtfully and fairly, holds the potential to deliver profound economic benefits, fostering substantial and widespread growth within a nation. By redistributing land from those who hold it disproportionately to previously marginalised communities, people gain access to vital assets that are crucial for economic participation and development. This access can empower individuals to engage in agriculture, start local businesses, and contribute to various sectors of the economy that were previously out of reach.

Nelson Mandela's assertion that "A nation should not be judged by how it treats its highest citizens, but its lowest ones"[162] highlights the essence of this process. It suggests that the true measure of a nation's progress and justice lies in how it uplifts its most disadvantaged members. In this context, land reform becomes a pivotal mechanism for addressing historical inequalities and providing opportunities for those at the bottom of the socio-economic ladder.

Redistributing land equitably allows marginalised communities to leverage these resources to their advantage. For instance, access to land enables smallholder farmers to invest in and enhance agricultural practices. They can improve productivity, diversify their crops, and adopt sustainable farming techniques. This not only increases their income but also contributes to national food security and economic stability. Additionally, by establishing local businesses, these individuals can stimulate local economies, create jobs, and drive innovation within their communities.

The ripple effects of such empowerment extend beyond the immediate economic gains. As more people gain access to productive

---

[162] United Nations, 'Standard Minimum Rules for the Treatment of Prisoners (the Nelson Mandela Rules)' (adopted 17 December 2015) UN Doc A/RES/70/175.

assets, there is a broader stimulation of economic activity. Increased investment in agriculture and local enterprises can lead to improved infrastructure, better access to services, and enhanced overall quality of life. This aligns with Mandela's vision of a nation where equitable treatment of its most vulnerable members fosters collective prosperity and growth.

The Increased agricultural productivity that often accompanies land redistribution represents a significant benefit of land expropriation. When previously marginalised communities gain access to land, smallholder farmers can engage in productive farming activities, which can lead to a more diverse and resilient agricultural sector. At the Regional People's Assembly of EFF in 2017 aptly noted, "Land reform is essential for the nation's development, as it is key to achieving the type of economic growth that will uplift all citizens." This statement underscores the importance of land reform in driving economic progress and highlights how essential it is for broader national development.

Access to land enables farmers to cultivate a variety of crops, raise livestock, and adopt modern farming techniques. These opportunities can dramatically enhance agricultural productivity and efficiency. For example, with secure land tenure, farmers can invest in improving their farming methods, such as adopting sustainable agricultural practices, using advanced technologies, and improving irrigation systems. These improvements lead to higher crop yields, better quality produce, and more efficient use of resources.

This boost in agricultural productivity has several positive outcomes. On a local level, it increases food production, which is crucial for meeting the nutritional needs of communities. Enhanced food security at the local level reduces dependency on food imports and stabilises local markets, which can protect consumers from price volatility. For countries where agriculture is a major economic activity, such as many developing nations, increased productivity translates directly into economic growth. By improving agricultural output, these countries can strengthen their economies, create jobs, and generate additional income from agricultural exports.

Moreover, a more productive agricultural sector contributes to national food security. When communities are empowered to produce their own food more efficiently, it lessens the reliance on external sources, which can be particularly important in times of global economic uncertainty or trade disruptions. This self-sufficiency helps to ensure that food supplies are more stable and less vulnerable to international market fluctuations.

Unlocking Economic Potential Through Equitable Land Distribution

In many developing countries, where agriculture forms the backbone of the economy, increased agricultural productivity can have a profound impact. It can stimulate economic growth by creating jobs in farming and related industries, such as processing and distribution. This, in turn, supports the development of rural areas, where agricultural activities are often concentrated. The ripple effects of improved agricultural productivity extend beyond the farm, influencing the broader economy by enhancing rural incomes, increasing spending power, and driving local economic development.[163]

In addition, when smallholder farmers have access to land, they can form cooperatives and engage in collective farming initiatives. These collaborations can lead to economies of scale, reduced production costs, and improved market access. By pooling resources and sharing knowledge, farmers can overcome some of the challenges associated with small-scale farming, such as limited access to capital and technology. These cooperative efforts can further amplify the benefits of land redistribution, leading to more substantial and widespread economic improvements.

Overall, the increased agricultural productivity resulting from land expropriation offers a range of economic benefits. It enhances food security, stimulates economic growth, supports rural development, and contributes to national prosperity. By providing previously marginalised

---

[163] C. Peter Timmer, *Agriculture and Pro-Poor Growth: An Asian Perspective* (Center for Global Development, USA 2005)

communities with access to land, governments can drive significant progress in agricultural sectors and broader economies, demonstrating the transformative potential of well-implemented land reform policies.

Land expropriation, when pursued with a focus on fairness and equity, can be a powerful tool for addressing and reducing economic inequality. Historically, land ownership has been disproportionately concentrated in the hands of a few privileged individuals or entities, creating and perpetuating significant disparities in wealth and opportunity. This concentration of land has often led to entrenched economic imbalances, with large segments of the population left without access to crucial resources that could enhance their economic prospects. By redistributing land more equitably, societies have the opportunity to correct these historical injustices and foster a more inclusive economic environment.

As Regional Secretary of the EFF in 2017 my assertion at the EFF's Regional People's Assembly that "Land reform is not just an issue of justice; it is a vital mechanism for alleviating poverty and inequality. It offers people the opportunity to improve their lives and create a better future." underscores the critical role of land reform in both addressing historical wrongs and promoting economic development. This statement highlights how land expropriation can serve as a mechanism for providing disenfranchised communities with the resources needed to improve their economic status. Access to land allows individuals and communities to participate more fully in economic activities, leading to wealth accumulation and enhanced economic opportunities.

The concentration of land ownership has historically resulted in significant disparities in wealth. When land is controlled by a small segment of the population, it limits the opportunities available to the broader populace, restricting their ability to engage in productive economic activities. By redistributing land to previously marginalised groups, governments can create a more balanced economic playing field. This redistribution allows more people to access productive assets, which can lead to increased participation in agriculture, local businesses, and other economic sectors.

Access to land enables previously disenfranchised individuals and communities to engage in activities that were previously out of reach. For instance, smallholder farmers who gain access to land can cultivate crops, raise livestock, and implement modern farming techniques. This not only enhances their productivity and efficiency but also contributes to national food security and economic stability. Additionally, access to land can empower individuals to start and expand local businesses, further stimulating economic activity and fostering local development.

My statement, "Land is an essential resource that can foster economic empowerment. Ensuring equitable access to land establishes the groundwork for a more just and equitable society," reinforces the idea that equitable land distribution is fundamental to achieving economic empowerment and social justice. Fair access to land provides individuals with the means to improve their economic circumstances, which can lead to greater social mobility and reduced poverty. By addressing the historical imbalances in land ownership, land reform contributes to creating a more just and equitable society where opportunities are more evenly distributed.

Equitable land distribution not only benefits individual landholders but also has broader economic implications. When more people gain access to land, they can contribute to a more diversified and resilient economy. For example, the establishment of small-scale agricultural operations and local businesses can create jobs, stimulate local markets, and foster innovation. This increased economic activity generates additional demand for goods and services, which can drive further economic growth and development. As a result, the positive effects of land redistribution extend beyond individual beneficiaries to impact the overall economy.

Moreover, equitable land distribution can help to address entrenched poverty. In many societies, poverty is closely linked to a lack of access to productive resources such as land. By providing access to land, governments can offer previously impoverished communities the means to improve their economic circumstances and reduce their reliance on external aid. This shift can lead to a more sustainable approach to poverty alleviation, as individuals and communities gain the tools to build better lives for themselves and contribute to their own economic development.

Land expropriation can also foster greater social mobility. When people have access to land and the economic opportunities it provides, they have the potential to improve their social and economic status. This upward mobility is essential for creating a dynamic and inclusive society where individuals can enhance their circumstances and contribute to the collective well-being of their communities. By providing a more equitable distribution of land, governments can help to create a society where opportunities are more accessible to all, reducing the barriers to economic advancement that have historically been faced by marginalised groups.

Land Access as a Catalyst for Rural Economic Growth

Access to land directly impacts agricultural productivity in several transformative ways. When land is expropriated and allocated to small-scale farmers, it can lead to significant improvements in farming efficiency, better management practices, and broader economic benefits. These changes are crucial for enhancing food security, promoting local economic development, and fostering sustainable agricultural practices.

Access to land allows farmers to implement improved land management practices that enhance soil fertility and crop yields. For instance, farmers can adopt crop rotation, a technique that involves alternating different types of crops in a specific sequence. This practice helps maintain soil health, reduce soil depletion, minimise pest infestations, and improve overall crop yields. Additionally, sustainable farming techniques, such as reduced tillage and organic farming, improve soil structure and fertility, leading to higher productivity. These practices not only enhance agricultural output but also contribute to long-term environmental sustainability.

Increased agricultural efficiency resulting from better land access has several positive outcomes. Firstly, it improves food security by increasing local food production. With higher productivity, small-scale farmers can grow a variety of crops, which helps meet the nutritional needs of local communities. This reduced reliance on imported goods helps to mitigate the risks associated with global market fluctuations and trade disruptions. Importing food can be both costly and unreliable, making domestic food production a more stable and sustainable solution.

Moreover, successful smallholder farms contribute to the economic development of rural areas. As these farms become more productive, they can generate additional income streams and create employment opportunities within their communities. For instance, increased agricultural output can lead to the development of local agro-processing industries, such as milling, canning, and packaging. These industries add value to raw produce and provide jobs for local residents. The expansion of these industries can stimulate economic activity and contribute to the overall development of rural areas.

In addition to creating jobs directly within agriculture, improved land access and agricultural productivity can have wider economic effects. As smallholder farms succeed and generate income, they create demand for goods and services, which benefits local businesses and services. This multiplier effect can lead to increased economic activity and growth within rural communities, further enhancing their overall economic well-being.

Furthermore, the increased productivity and efficiency from land access can contribute to a more resilient agricultural sector. By diversifying crop production and adopting modern farming techniques, small-scale farmers can better withstand environmental and economic shocks. This resilience is particularly important in regions prone to climate variability and market fluctuations, where traditional agricultural practices may not be sufficient to ensure stability.

Access to land also encourages rural entrepreneurship. When individuals have secure land tenure, they are more likely to invest in and develop agricultural enterprises. This can include expanding existing farms, starting new agricultural ventures, or diversifying into related industries, such as agro-tourism or organic farming. The growth of rural entrepreneurship fosters economic innovation and provides additional income streams for communities, further contributing to economic development.

Incorporating sustainable farming practices is another significant benefit of improved land access. Smallholder farmers who have secure land tenure are more likely to engage in practices that enhance environmental sustainability. Techniques such as organic farming, agroforestry, and integrated pest management help maintain ecological balance, conserve natural resources, and reduce the environmental impact of agriculture. Sustainable farming practices not only improve productivity but also contribute to long-term environmental health.

Improved access to land and enhanced agricultural productivity can increase the resilience of farming communities to economic and environmental shocks. By diversifying crops and adopting modern farming practices, smallholder farmers can better withstand fluctuations in market prices, climate variability, and other challenges. This resilience is crucial in areas prone to extreme weather events or economic instability, as it helps communities adapt and recover more effectively.

Access to land empowers individuals and communities by providing them with a stake in their economic future. Secure land tenure fosters a sense of ownership and responsibility, encouraging people to invest in and improve their land. This empowerment can lead to greater social stability, as communities that have access to land and economic opportunities are more likely to invest in their own development and contribute positively to society.

Land expropriation has the potential to act as a powerful catalyst for rural development, bringing substantial economic growth and improvements in living standards to previously neglected areas. When land is redistributed, it often leads to the creation of new business opportunities, which in turn stimulates job creation and advances infrastructure and services in these communities.

The process of land redistribution empowers smallholder farmers and local entrepreneurs by providing them with the resources they need to establish and expand their businesses. This empowerment is a significant boost to agricultural productivity and broader economic development. As individuals and communities gain access to land, they are able to invest in their agricultural activities, start new ventures, and engage in economic activities that were previously beyond their reach. This entrepreneurial energy fosters economic dynamism and resilience within rural areas.

The Interplay between Infrastructure and Economic Development

Improved infrastructure is another crucial benefit of land expropriation. As new businesses and farms are established, there is often a need for better transportation networks, including roads and bridges, to facilitate the movement of goods and services. Enhanced infrastructure not only supports agricultural and business activities but also improves access to essential services and resources. For example, better roads can enhance connectivity, making it easier for farmers to reach markets and for businesses to distribute products. This improved infrastructure contributes to the overall efficiency of the local economy and supports further economic growth.

The rise of new economic activities in rural areas frequently leads to enhanced community services. As local economies expand, there is a greater demand for educational and healthcare facilities. New businesses and increased economic activity can lead to the development of better schools, which offer improved educational opportunities for children and adults. Similarly, the expansion of healthcare services ensures better access to medical care, which contributes to improved health outcomes for rural populations. This development of educational and healthcare facilities is essential for raising the overall quality of life in rural communities.

The relationship between economic development and infrastructure improvement is mutually reinforcing. As rural areas develop economically, there is a corresponding increase in investment in community services and infrastructure. Conversely, enhanced infrastructure and services support further economic growth by creating a more conducive environment for business and investment. This creates a positive feedback loop where economic development and quality of life improvements reinforce each other, leading to a cycle of continued growth and development.

Land expropriation also encourages rural entrepreneurship. When individuals have secure land tenure, they are more likely to invest in and develop agricultural and business enterprises. This investment can involve expanding existing farms, starting new agricultural ventures, or diversifying into related industries, such as agro-tourism or organic farming. The growth of rural entrepreneurship stimulates economic innovation and provides additional income streams, further contributing to the development of rural areas.

Moreover, improved access to land facilitates the adoption of sustainable farming practices. Farmers with secure land tenure are more likely to invest in long-term soil and environmental management practices, such as organic farming, agroforestry, and integrated pest management. These practices help to enhance soil fertility, conserve natural resources, and reduce the environmental impact of agriculture. Sustainable farming practices contribute to the long-term viability and resilience of rural economies by promoting environmental stewardship and resource conservation.

Beyond economic and environmental benefits, land expropriation can foster social cohesion and stability. By providing previously marginalised communities with access to land and economic opportunities, land redistribution helps integrate these communities into the broader economic and social fabric. This inclusion fosters a sense of ownership and community pride, which can lead to greater social stability and collective investment in community development. The integration of marginalised communities into the economic mainstream helps address historical inequalities and injustices, contributing to a more equitable society.

The impact of land expropriation extends to addressing historical disparities in access to resources and opportunities. Many rural areas have experienced long-standing inequalities that have hindered their development. By redistributing land, governments can work towards rectifying these imbalances and ensuring that all individuals and communities have the chance to participate in and benefit from economic growth. This process of addressing historical injustices through land reform is a crucial step towards building a more inclusive and equitable society.

As the benefits of land expropriation continue to unfold, it becomes evident that the process not only enhances economic opportunities and infrastructure but also strengthens social and environmental foundations. The empowerment of individuals and communities through land access contributes to a more dynamic and resilient rural economy, fostering sustainable development and improved quality of life.

Enhancing Investment Attraction through Secure Land Reform

A well-implemented land reform programme can play a crucial role in attracting investment by creating a stable and predictable environment where property rights are secure. Investors are particularly drawn to environments where they can be assured that their investments are protected, and clear land ownership and usage rights are essential to achieving this stability.

When a country establishes clear and fair land ownership structures, it enhances its appeal to both local and international investors. The presence of well-defined land rights reduces the risk of disputes and uncertainties, making it easier for investors to commit resources with confidence. For instance, investors in agriculture often require long-term security over land to justify their investments in improving soil quality, purchasing advanced equipment, and adopting modern farming techniques. When land tenure is secure, investors are more likely to invest in these improvements, leading to increased agricultural productivity and sustainability.

In addition to agriculture, clear land ownership structures are vital for attracting investment in infrastructure projects. Infrastructure development, such as roads, bridges, and utilities, often requires significant capital investment and long-term planning. Investors are more likely to commit to such projects if they are confident that their land rights will be upheld and protected. This assurance enables investors to plan and execute large-scale infrastructure projects that contribute to overall economic development by improving connectivity, enhancing trade, and facilitating business operations.

The real estate sector also benefits from secure land tenure. Investors in real estate are more inclined to develop residential, commercial, and industrial properties in areas where land ownership is clear and secure. This investment leads to the expansion of urban areas, the creation of new commercial hubs, and the development of residential neighbourhoods. Such growth stimulates local economies by generating employment opportunities, increasing property values, and enhancing the availability of goods and services.

Furthermore, the stability provided by secure land tenure fosters investment in various sectors, including tourism and manufacturing. For example, investors looking to develop tourist resorts or cultural attractions require certainty about land rights to proceed with their plans. Similarly, manufacturing facilities often need secure land to build and expand their operations. By ensuring that land ownership and usage rights are clearly defined, governments can attract investment in these sectors, leading to increased economic activity and diversification.

In addition to attracting direct investment, clear land ownership structures contribute to the overall business environment by reducing the likelihood of land-related conflicts. Disputes over land can create significant barriers to investment, as they introduce uncertainty and risk. By addressing these issues through effective land reform, governments can create a more conducive environment for business operations and investment.

The positive impact of secure land tenure extends beyond the immediate economic benefits. It also promotes social stability and confidence in the legal system. When individuals and businesses have confidence in the protection of their land rights, it fosters a sense of security and stability within the community. This, in turn, contributes to a more predictable and orderly investment climate, where businesses and investors feel more comfortable making long-term commitments.

A well-executed land reform programme that establishes clear and secure land ownership structures is instrumental in attracting investment. By providing stability and reducing the risk of land-related disputes, such reforms enhance a country's appeal to investors, stimulate economic activity, and support growth in key sectors such as agriculture, infrastructure, real estate, tourism, and manufacturing.

When aligned with sustainable practices, land expropriation can significantly contribute to environmental sustainability. Effective land management and conservation efforts play a crucial role in preventing overexploitation and degradation of natural resources. Integrating environmental considerations into land reform policies ensures that land is used in a manner that supports long-term ecological balance and resource conservation.

Properly managed land expropriation programmes can incorporate sustainable land use practices that address environmental concerns. For instance, land reform initiatives that include provisions for reforestation and conservation agriculture can enhance the ecological health of the land. Reforestation efforts help restore deforested areas, improve soil quality, and sequester carbon dioxide, which mitigates the effects of climate change. By reintroducing native vegetation and creating protected areas, these initiatives contribute to the preservation of biodiversity and the resilience of ecosystems.

Conservation agriculture is another key aspect of sustainable land management. This approach involves practices such as reduced tillage, crop rotation, and cover cropping, which improve soil health and reduce erosion. These methods help maintain soil fertility, enhance water retention, and reduce the need for chemical inputs, leading to more sustainable agricultural practices. By integrating conservation agriculture into land reform policies, governments can support farming methods that are both environmentally friendly and economically viable.

Land expropriation that prioritises environmental stewardship also involves protecting natural habitats and wildlife. Designating certain areas as conservation zones or protected reserves prevents land from being used in ways that could harm delicate ecosystems. This approach ensures that critical habitats for wildlife are preserved, contributing to the maintenance of ecological balance and the protection of endangered species.

Incorporating environmental considerations into land reform policies not only addresses immediate ecological concerns but also promotes long-term sustainability. By establishing guidelines and regulations that support sustainable land use, governments can ensure that land reform efforts contribute to the broader goals of environmental protection and resource conservation. This proactive approach helps to prevent negative environmental impacts and supports the development of resilient ecosystems that can adapt to changing conditions.

The alignment of land expropriation with sustainable practices also supports community engagement and education. When communities are involved in and educated about sustainable land management practices, they are more likely to adopt and support these practices. This involvement can include training on sustainable farming techniques, community-based conservation projects, and participatory decision-making processes. By fostering a sense of ownership and responsibility, these initiatives can lead to more effective and widespread implementation of sustainable land use practices.

When land expropriation programmes incorporate sustainable land management practices, they can significantly contribute to environmental sustainability. By integrating reforestation, conservation agriculture, and habitat protection into land reform policies, governments can support long-term ecological balance and resource conservation. These efforts help mitigate climate change, preserve biodiversity, and promote responsible land use, benefiting both current and future generations.

Economic stability and social cohesion are deeply interconnected, and land expropriation can be a powerful tool in strengthening both. By addressing historical injustices and providing equitable access to resources, land reform initiatives can contribute significantly to a more just and stable society.

The Role of Land Reform in Promoting Social Equity

Historically, land ownership has been a central issue in many societies, often reflecting and perpetuating socio-economic inequalities. In numerous cases, land dispossession and unequal distribution have led to significant disparities in wealth and opportunity. Land expropriation, when executed fairly and thoughtfully, offers a means to correct these imbalances by redistributing land to those who have been historically marginalised or dispossessed. This process of rectifying historical wrongs helps to build a foundation for social equity and inclusion, addressing long-standing grievances and fostering a sense of justice among affected communities.

The provision of equitable access to land not only addresses past Injustices but also creates opportunities for economic advancement. Secure land tenure allows individuals and families to invest in their land and businesses with confidence. For example, farmers with stable land rights are more likely to invest in improving their agricultural practices, adopting new technologies, and expanding their operations. Similarly, those who receive land through reform programmes may establish new businesses, contribute to local economies, and create jobs. This economic empowerment leads to increased prosperity within communities and enhances overall economic stability.

Furthermore, secure land tenure fosters community engagement and investment. When individuals feel confident in their land rights, they are more likely to invest time, resources, and effort into improving their properties and supporting community initiatives. This investment can manifest in various ways, including the development of local infrastructure, participation in community projects, and support for local businesses. Such engagement strengthens social ties and fosters a sense of collective responsibility and ownership, which is crucial for social cohesion.

Social stability is further reinforced when people perceive that they have fair opportunities to improve their lives. Land reform programmes that provide equitable access to resources help to bridge socio-economic gaps and reduce disparities between different groups. When citizens see that they have a genuine chance to succeed and enhance their living conditions, they are more likely to contribute positively to their communities. This inclusivity and fairness promote a sense of belonging and reduce feelings of resentment or alienation, which can otherwise lead to social unrest and instability.

Addressing land-related grievances through reform also plays a key role in reducing conflict and tensions. Land disputes have historically been a major source of social discord and violence. By implementing transparent and equitable land reform processes, governments can mitigate these conflicts and promote reconciliation. Fair land distribution helps to resolve disputes over land ownership and use, reducing the potential for social and political tensions. This approach fosters a more harmonious society where land-related issues are addressed through peaceful and constructive means.

Additionally, land expropriation that incorporates sustainable land management practices further contributes to social stability. Sustainable land use practices, such as conservation agriculture, reforestation, and habitat protection, support long-term environmental health and resilience. When land reform includes provisions for environmental stewardship, it not only benefits the natural environment but also enhances the quality of life for communities. Healthy ecosystems provide essential resources, such as clean water and fertile soil, which are crucial for community well-being and economic stability.

Involving communities in the land reform process is also essential for ensuring its success and fostering social cohesion. Engaging local stakeholders in decision-making and implementation helps to ensure that land reform policies are responsive to community needs and priorities. This participatory approach promotes a sense of ownership and accountability, increasing the likelihood of successful outcomes and long-term sustainability.

Land expropriation that addresses historical injustices and provides equitable access to resources can significantly enhance economic stability and social cohesion. By rectifying past wrongs, empowering communities, and fostering inclusive development, land reform contributes to a more just and stable society. Secure land tenure, fair access to resources, and community engagement all play a crucial role in building a resilient social fabric and reducing conflicts. Through thoughtful and equitable land reform, societies can create a foundation for sustained economic growth and social harmony.

Conclusion

In conclusion, land expropriation, when executed with fairness and efficiency, offers a profound range of economic benefits that can drive transformative change in societies. Properly managed land reform initiatives have the potential to stimulate significant economic growth by redistributing land to previously marginalised communities, thereby unlocking their potential to contribute to the economy. Access to land can provide these communities with the means to invest in agriculture, start businesses, and engage in productive activities that boost local economies and foster broader economic development.

Reducing socio-economic inequalities is another critical benefit of land expropriation. Historically, land ownership has been a major determinant of wealth and opportunity, with many communities historically disenfranchised and excluded from access to land. By redistributing land more equitably, land reform addresses these historical injustices, enabling previously excluded groups to gain access to valuable resources. This redistribution helps to narrow the wealth gap and create a more balanced and inclusive economy, where the benefits of growth are shared more widely.

Enhancing agricultural productivity is a key advantage of land reform. Secure land tenure allows smallholder farmers to invest in their land and adopt improved farming practices, leading to increased productivity and efficiency. When farmers have confidence in their land rights, they are more likely to invest in modern agricultural techniques, which can result in higher crop yields and greater food security. This boost in agricultural productivity not only benefits local communities but also contributes to national food security and reduces dependence on imported goods.

Driving rural development is another significant benefit of land expropriation. By redistributing land, new business opportunities often emerge, leading to job creation and improvements in infrastructure and services. The establishment of smallholder farms and local enterprises can stimulate investment in rural areas, enhancing the availability of essential services such as roads, schools, and healthcare facilities. This development not only improves the quality of life in rural communities but also contributes to overall economic growth.

Attracting investment is a crucial outcome of well-executed land reform. Investors seek stable environments where property rights are clear and secure. By establishing transparent and equitable land ownership structures, countries can enhance their attractiveness to both local and international investors. Secure land tenure provides the confidence needed for investors to commit resources to various sectors, including agriculture, infrastructure, and real estate. This influx of investment supports economic diversification and long-term development.

Environmental sustainability is another important benefit of land expropriation when aligned with sustainable practices. Incorporating environmental considerations into land reform policies ensures that land is used responsibly, supporting long-term ecological balance. Sustainable land management practices, such as reforestation, conservation agriculture, and habitat protection, help to preserve natural resources and mitigate the effects of climate change. These practices not only benefit the environment but also support the livelihoods of communities dependent on these resources.

Social stability is enhanced through land expropriation by addressing historical grievances and providing equitable access to resources. When communities perceive that they have fair opportunities to improve their lives, it fosters a sense of inclusion and belonging. Secure land tenure reduces the risk of conflicts over land disputes and promotes community engagement. By addressing past injustices and reducing socio-economic disparities, land reform contributes to a more cohesive and stable society.

The perspectives of African political leaders and figures like Julius Malema highlight the transformative potential of land reform in achieving these diverse goals. Their observations point out the essential importance of land expropriation in rectifying historical injustices, encouraging economic growth, and advancing social justice. By implementing land reform thoughtfully and inclusively, societies can harness its power as a tool for advancing both economic and social progress. Through equitable distribution of resources and sustainable practices, land expropriation can help create a more just, prosperous, and resilient future for all.

9. THE POSITIVE IMPACT OF INTERNATIONAL INFLUENCE ON LAND REFORM

Land reform in South Africa is a multifaceted and complex process, profoundly shaped by various international influences. This includes international perspectives on land rights, the impact of foreign aid, the role of global organisations, and the effects of foreign investment. Each of these elements has played a crucial role in shaping the country's efforts to achieve a fair and equitable distribution of land, reflecting the broader global discourse on justice and human rights.

The global human rights movement has been a significant driver In shaping South Africa's land reform policies. International perspectives on land rights have increasingly recognised land as a crucial element of human dignity and justice. The United Nations (UN), through its conventions and resolutions, has established a framework that underscores land rights as essential to achieving economic, social, and cultural rights. The International Covenant on Economic, Social and Cultural Rights (ICESCR), for instance, articulates the right to adequate housing and protection from forced displacement. These international norms and standards have served as benchmarks for South Africa, guiding its land reform policies to align with global principles of justice and equity.[164]

The UN's involvement in land reform has been both broad and specific. At a broad level, the UN has played a key role in promoting global discussions on land rights, influencing national policies through international agreements and advocacy. Specific initiatives, such as those led by the UN Habitat programme, have focused on improving secure

---

[164] M Aliber and R Mokoena, *'The Land Question in Contemporary South Africa'* (HSRC Press).

land tenure and access to land for disadvantaged communities. These programmes have provided practical support to South Africa, helping to implement policies that address historical injustices and promote social inclusion.

Foreign aid has been another critical factor in advancing South Africa's land reform agenda. International organisations, particularly the World Bank, have provided substantial financial resources and technical expertise. This support has been instrumental in overcoming some of the financial and logistical challenges faced by the South African government. For example, funding from international bodies has facilitated the development of land reform policies, supported the implementation of land redistribution programmes, and enhanced land administration systems.

Beyond financial resources, the technical expertise provided by foreign donors has been vital in shaping effective land reform strategies. This assistance has included guidance on best practices for land redistribution, support for developing land tenure systems, and help in establishing mechanisms for dispute resolution. By incorporating these best practices and expert recommendations, South Africa has been able to refine its land reform processes and improve their effectiveness.

Foreign aid has also contributed significantly to building institutional capacity within South Africa. Training and knowledge transfer initiatives funded by international partners have strengthened the skills and capabilities of local officials and organisations involved in land reform. This capacity building has been crucial for ensuring that land reform policies are not only well-designed but also effectively implemented. The ability of local institutions to manage and oversee land reform initiatives has a direct impact on the success and sustainability of these programmes.

Global organisations, beyond the UN, have also played a substantial role in the land reform process in South Africa. These organisations provide platforms for dialogue and collaboration, facilitating international cooperation and knowledge exchange. For example, the International Land Coalition (ILC) and other global entities have worked to advocate for land rights and promote effective land governance. Their involvement has helped to align South Africa's land reform efforts with international best practices and standards.

Regional organisations, such as the African Union (AU), have also had an impact on South Africa's land reform discourse. The AU has supported policies aimed at improving land governance and promoting equitable land distribution across the continent. This regional perspective has provided South Africa with additional frameworks and insights for addressing its land reform challenges. The AU's initiatives have encouraged member states, including South Africa, to adopt policies that address land issues in a manner that is consistent with regional and continental goals.

Foreign investment has introduced a new dimension to South Africa's land reform landscape. The influx of international capital has spurred economic development and created job opportunities, particularly in sectors such as agriculture and infrastructure. This investment has supported the development of productive land use and enhanced the country's economic growth. For example, foreign investors have contributed to the expansion of agricultural activities, which has had a positive impact on local economies and food security.

However, the presence of foreign investment has also presented challenges. One of the primary concerns has been ensuring that the benefits of investment are equitably shared and that local communities are not marginalised. The integration of foreign investment into the land reform process requires careful management to balance the interests of investors with the need for fair land distribution. Ensuring that land reform policies adequately address the needs of local communities while also accommodating investment interests is a complex task that requires ongoing attention.

The World Bank's Impact on South Africa's Land Reform

The interaction between foreign investment and land reform also highlights the importance of effective land governance. Transparent and fair land allocation processes are essential to ensure that investment does not exacerbate existing inequalities or lead to new forms of land-related disputes. The involvement of international investors in land reform necessitates robust regulatory frameworks that safeguard the rights of local communities and ensure that investment contributes to equitable development.

Overall, the interplay of international perspectives, foreign aid, global organisations, and foreign investment has been instrumental in shaping South Africa's land reform efforts. These external forces have collectively driven the progress of land reform initiatives, contributing to the country's pursuit of a more equitable and just land distribution system. The influence of these international factors underscores the interconnected nature of global and local efforts in addressing land reform challenges.

As South Africa continues to navigate its land reform journey, the impact of these international influences will remain significant. The ongoing engagement with global perspectives, the continued support of foreign aid, the collaboration with global and regional organisations, and the management of foreign investment will all play critical roles in shaping the future of land reform in South Africa. Balancing these influences with domestic priorities and ensuring that land reform efforts achieve their intended outcomes will be essential for the success of South Africa's land reform agenda.

The World Bank's involvement in South Africa's land reform process has played a pivotal role in shaping and advancing the country's efforts towards a more equitable land distribution system. This involvement has been crucial in several key areas, including the modernisation of land administration systems, the enhancement of land tenure security, and the promotion of equitable land distribution. The impacts of these initiatives are evident in the increased stability and transparency within South Africa's land management system, which are essential for achieving effective land reform.

One of the central focuses of the World Bank's intervention has been the modernisation of land administration systems. Prior to these interventions, South Africa's land administration faced significant challenges. The land registries were outdated, management processes were inefficient, and there were widespread disputes over land ownership. These issues were largely a legacy of historical land dispossessions and a lack of comprehensive and accurate land records. In response to these challenges, the World Bank has funded projects aimed at upgrading land registries and improving land management efficiency. The modernisation process has involved the digitisation of land records and the implementation of advanced technologies and best practices for land registration. By creating a more accurate and accessible system of land administration, these upgrades have greatly reduced disputes over land ownership. For previously marginalised communities, the enhanced registries have made it easier to secure land rights, which is crucial for both economic stability and social inclusion. The streamlined process has fostered a more transparent and reliable framework for managing land transactions and ownership claims, thereby increasing confidence in the system and reducing the potential for conflicts.

In addition to modernising land administration systems, the World Bank has made significant contributions to strengthening land tenure security. Historically, many communities in South Africa lacked formal recognition of their land rights, which undermined their ability to invest in and manage their land effectively. The World Bank has supported initiatives aimed at providing formal land titles to these communities. This formalisation process has been transformative, offering legal recognition of land ownership and thereby enhancing land tenure security. With secure land tenure, communities are better positioned to make long-term investments in their land, leading to improved agricultural productivity and greater economic stability. Furthermore, formal land titles contribute to social cohesion by providing communities with a sense of ownership and stability. This empowerment has also helped to address historical injustices, promoting a fairer and more inclusive land distribution system.

Promoting equitable land distribution has been another significant area of focus for the World Bank. Land reform in South Africa has grappled with the challenge of addressing historical disparities in land ownership. Many disadvantaged groups have had limited access to land resources, a legacy of past injustices. The World Bank has supported policies and programmes designed to ensure fair access to land, particularly for these disadvantaged groups. This support has included backing initiatives that aim to rectify historical injustices by redistributing land to those who have been historically excluded or marginalised. By targeting disadvantaged groups and working towards a more balanced distribution of land resources, the World Bank has helped to advance the goal of achieving greater equity within South Africa's land reform process.

The positive outcomes of the World Bank's projects are evident In the increased stability and transparency within South Africa's land management system. The modernisation of land administration systems has resulted in a more reliable and efficient framework for managing land records, which is crucial for effective land reform. Enhanced land tenure security has empowered communities, encouraged investment, and led to greater economic stability and social cohesion. The promotion of equitable land distribution has contributed to addressing historical injustices and achieving a fairer distribution of land resources. Overall, the World Bank's involvement has been instrumental in advancing South Africa's land reform efforts, creating a more inclusive and effective land management system.

Beyond the immediate impacts of its projects, the World Bank's contribution has influenced broader land reform policies and practices in South Africa. The experience and expertise provided through World Bank-funded initiatives have informed and shaped national policies, leading to more effective and comprehensive land reform strategies. This influence has been crucial in driving progress towards a more equitable and just land distribution system, aligning with global standards of land governance and social justice.

The World Bank's role extends to facilitating dialogue and collaboration on land reform issues. Through its support, the World Bank has helped to create platforms for national and international stakeholders to engage in discussions about land reform. This dialogue has been essential for developing a shared understanding of land issues and for identifying and implementing effective solutions. The World Bank's involvement in fostering such discussions has contributed to a more coordinated and cohesive approach to land reform, involving a wide range of stakeholders, including government agencies, local communities, and international partners.

Additionally, the World Bank's support has included efforts to build institutional capacity within South Africa. Training and knowledge transfer initiatives funded by the World Bank have strengthened the skills and capabilities of local officials and organisations involved in land reform. This capacity building has been vital for ensuring that land reform policies are not only well-designed but also effectively implemented. The ability of local institutions to manage and oversee land reform initiatives directly impacts the success and sustainability of these programmes. By enhancing the capabilities of local stakeholders, the World Bank has helped to create a more robust and effective framework for land reform.

The impact of the World Bank's involvement is also reflected in the broader economic and social benefits that have arisen from improved land management and distribution. For example, increased land tenure security and more equitable land distribution have led to greater agricultural productivity and more sustainable land use practices. This has had positive implications for food security and local economic development. Furthermore, by addressing historical injustices and promoting social inclusion, the World Bank's projects have contributed to a more cohesive and stable society.

However, it is important to acknowledge that the process of land reform is complex and multifaceted, and challenges remain. While the World Bank's involvement has yielded positive outcomes, there are ongoing issues related to land reform that need to be addressed. These include ensuring that land reform policies are effectively implemented, addressing remaining disparities in land access, and continuing to support communities in adapting to new land management systems. The World Bank's support will likely continue to be an important factor in addressing these challenges and advancing the goals of land reform in South Africa.

In summary, the World Bank's involvement in South Africa's land reform process has been extensive and impactful. Through its support for modernising land administration systems, enhancing land tenure security, and promoting equitable land distribution, the World Bank has played a crucial role in advancing South Africa's land reform efforts. The positive outcomes of these initiatives highlight the importance of international support and collaboration in achieving effective land reform and addressing historical injustices. As South Africa continues to navigate its land reform journey, the World Bank's contributions will remain significant in shaping the future of land management and distribution in the country. The ongoing engagement with global perspectives, the continued support of foreign aid, and the collaboration with international organisations will all play critical roles in shaping the success of South Africa's land reform agenda.

NGOs and International Organisations on South Africa's Land Reform

The role of non-governmental organisations (NGOs) and international organisations in South Africa's land reform process has been extensive and influential. Their involvement has been crucial in advancing land reform by raising awareness about land rights issues, advocating for policy changes, and facilitating dialogue between communities and policymakers. This comprehensive engagement has significantly shaped land reform policies and helped address the historical injustices and challenges associated with land distribution in South Africa.[165]

NGOs such as Oxfam and ActionAid have been at the forefront of

---

[165] Aliber and Mokoena, 'The Land Question in Contemporary South Africa' (n164)

raising awareness about land rights issues and advocating for necessary policy changes. Their advocacy work has played a vital role in highlighting the needs and concerns of affected communities, thereby influencing land reform policies. One of the primary ways in which NGOs have raised awareness is through rigorous research and the publication of detailed reports on land rights and land reform issues. Organisations like Oxfam and ActionAid conduct comprehensive studies that document the extent of land dispossession, the socio-economic impacts on displaced communities, and the deficiencies in existing land reform policies. These reports often include empirical data, case studies, and personal testimonies that provide a nuanced understanding of the challenges faced by marginalised groups. By making this information publicly available, these organisations help to illuminate the scale of the problem and the urgent need for effective land reform measures.

The publication of such reports garners significant media attention, which amplifies the message and puts additional pressure on policymakers to address land rights issues. Media coverage of these reports helps to inform the broader public about the complexities of land reform and the importance of addressing historical injustices. This increased public awareness can lead to greater support for policy changes and can drive political action to address land rights concerns.

In addition to research and publication, NGOs engage in grassroots advocacy to build awareness and mobilise support for land reform. These organisations work directly with affected communities to educate individuals about their land rights and the importance of land reform. They organise community meetings, workshops, and public demonstrations to facilitate discussions about land issues and to rally support for policy changes. By empowering communities to actively participate in advocacy efforts, NGOs help to ensure that the voices of those directly impacted by land dispossession are heard and considered in the policy-making process.

Grassroots advocacy also involves working with local leaders and community-based organisations to strengthen their capacity to advocate for land reform. NGOs provide training and resources to help these local actors effectively engage with policymakers and advocate for their communities' needs. This capacity-building approach ensures that advocacy efforts are sustained and that communities have the tools they need to effectively influence land reform policies.

NGOs also play a critical role in lobbying for policy changes at both national and international levels. Through lobbying efforts, these organisations engage with government officials, legislators, and international bodies to advocate for reforms that address land rights issues. They present evidence-based arguments, share successful case studies from other countries, and highlight the social and economic benefits of land reform. By engaging in lobbying efforts, NGOs help to ensure that land reform policies are not only responsive to the needs of affected communities but also aligned with global standards of human rights and social justice.

The advocacy work of NGOs Is complemented by their efforts to build coalitions and networks with other organisations and stakeholders. By collaborating with other NGOs, community groups, and international organisations, these advocacy efforts are amplified and made more effective. The formation of coalitions helps to pool resources, share expertise, and coordinate strategies, leading to more comprehensive and impactful advocacy initiatives.

International organisations have also played a crucial role in facilitating dialogue and mediation between communities and policymakers. Their involvement as neutral intermediaries has been essential in ensuring that the voices of affected people are heard and considered in the policy-making process. One of the key functions of international organisations in this regard has been to organise and mediate multi-stakeholder dialogues. These dialogues bring together a diverse range of participants, including community representatives, government officials, NGOs, and other stakeholders, to discuss land reform challenges and potential solutions. The structured nature of these dialogues allows for open and transparent discussions, where different perspectives can be shared and debated. This inclusive approach helps to build consensus on land reform issues and ensures that policies are more responsive to the needs of all stakeholders.

The facilitation of dialogue by international organisations often involves creating safe and neutral spaces where stakeholders can engage in constructive discussions. These spaces are designed to foster open communication, encourage collaboration, and address potential conflicts. By providing a platform for dialogue, international organisations help to bridge the gap between communities and policymakers, facilitating a more collaborative approach to land reform.

In addition to organising dialogues, international organisations provide technical assistance and support for mediation processes. This support includes facilitating workshops, training sessions, and capacity-building activities that help stakeholders develop the skills necessary for effective negotiation and conflict resolution. By strengthening the ability of communities and policymakers to engage in constructive dialogue, international organisations contribute to more inclusive and equitable land reform policies.

The Involvement of international organisations in dialogue and mediation also includes efforts to ensure that the voices of marginalised and vulnerable groups are included in the policy-making process. This involves working with community organisations to amplify the voices of those who may not have direct access to decision-makers. International organisations often provide platforms for these groups to share their experiences and concerns, ensuring that their perspectives are represented in discussions about land reform. This approach helps to address power Imbalances and ensures that land reform policies are more inclusive and equitable.

The Impact of dialogue facilitation by international organisations is evident in the development of more responsive and inclusive land reform policies. Through their efforts, these organisations have helped to create opportunities for collaborative problem-solving and have contributed to the development of policies that are better aligned with the needs of affected communities. The emphasis on inclusive dialogue ensures that policies are grounded in the experiences and perspectives of those most affected by land issues, leading to more effective and equitable outcomes.

Furthermore, the engagement of international organisations in dialogue and mediation has contributed to greater transparency and accountability in the land reform process. By facilitating open discussions and involving a wide range of stakeholders, these organisations help to ensure that land reform efforts are conducted in a manner that is open and accountable to the public. This increased transparency helps to build trust in the land reform process and encourages greater public support for policy initiatives.

While the involvement of NGOs and international organisations has been instrumental in advancing land reform, several challenges and considerations need to be addressed. One of the primary challenges is ensuring that advocacy efforts and dialogue processes lead to meaningful and sustainable policy changes. Despite the significant contributions of these organisations, land reform policies can be slow to implement, and progress may be hindered by political and bureaucratic obstacles.

Another challenge is the need for continued engagement and support for affected communities throughout the land reform process. While advocacy and dialogue are crucial, it is essential to ensure that communities have the resources and support they need to effectively participate in and benefit from land reform initiatives. This includes addressing capacity-building needs, providing technical assistance, and ensuring that communities have access to information and resources.

Additionally, the impact of international organisations and NGOs can vary depending on the specific context and dynamics of land reform in different regions. The effectiveness of their involvement depends on factors such as the level of political will, the existing legal and institutional framework, and the capacity of local stakeholders. It is important for these organisations to adapt their strategies to the local context and work collaboratively with national and local partners to achieve the desired outcomes.

The involvement of NGOs and international organisations in South Africa's land reform process has been pivotal in advancing the goals of land rights and equitable land distribution. Their comprehensive engagement, ranging from advocacy and awareness-raising to facilitating dialogue and mediation, has significantly influenced land reform policies and helped address the historical injustices and challenges associated with land distribution. Their contributions underscore the importance of international support and collaboration in achieving meaningful and sustainable land reform outcomes.

The Positive Impact of Foreign Investment on South Africa's Land Reform

Foreign investment has had a substantial impact on land reform in South Africa, bringing with it a range of positive effects when approached with responsibility and foresight. These benefits extend across various facets of land management and economic development, encompassing the injection of resources and expertise, infrastructure development, and job creation. The interplay between international investment and land reform illustrates how strategic partnerships and thoughtful implementation can advance both economic growth and social equity.

One of the primary advantages of foreign investment is the infusion of resources and expertise into land management and development projects. International investors often bring advanced technologies, innovative practices, and substantial financial capital that can significantly enhance the productivity and efficiency of various sectors. In the agricultural sector, for example, foreign investment has led to the introduction of modern farming techniques such as precision agriculture, which uses data and technology to optimise crop yields. These advancements not only improve the efficiency of farming operations but also contribute to better resource management, ensuring that land is used sustainably and effectively. This enhanced productivity directly supports the goals of land reform by helping to increase food security and provide economic opportunities for local farmers.

Moreover, the expertise that international investors bring can lead to the development of more sophisticated land management systems. These systems often incorporate best practices from around the world, including advanced soil management, integrated pest control, and climate-smart agriculture techniques. By implementing these practices, foreign investments can help to improve soil health, reduce environmental degradation, and increase the resilience of agricultural systems to climate change. This support is crucial for ensuring that land reform efforts are not only focused on redistribution but also on sustainable land use that benefits current and future generations.

In addition to enhancing land management practices, foreign investment plays a crucial role in infrastructure development. Investments in infrastructure such as roads, irrigation systems, and storage facilities are essential for supporting land development and facilitating economic activities. Improved road networks, for instance, enable farmers to transport their produce more efficiently to markets, reducing transportation costs and increasing their access to broader markets. This enhanced connectivity can lead to higher revenues for farmers and greater economic integration of rural areas into national and global economies.

Investment in irrigation systems is another critical area where foreign investment can have a significant impact. Reliable irrigation infrastructure ensures that crops receive consistent and adequate water supplies, which is essential for maintaining high productivity levels. By reducing dependence on erratic rainfall and improving water management, irrigation systems contribute to more stable and predictable agricultural outputs. This stability is beneficial for both smallholder and commercial farmers, helping to secure livelihoods and promote agricultural growth.

Storage facilities are equally important, as they allow farmers to store their produce safely and sell it when market conditions are more favourable. Investments in modern storage facilities can help to reduce post-harvest losses and improve the overall efficiency of the agricultural supply chain. This not only benefits individual farmers but also contributes to the stability and resilience of the agricultural sector as a whole.

Foreign investment also contributes to job creation, which has a profound impact on economic development and local livelihoods. By establishing new businesses, expanding existing operations, or undertaking development projects, international investors create a range of employment opportunities across different sectors. These job opportunities span various levels, from agricultural work to construction and administrative roles, providing diverse employment prospects for local populations. The creation of jobs helps to stimulate economic growth, reduce poverty, and enhance the overall standard of living in affected areas.

Job creation through foreign investment can also have multiplier effects on local economies. For example, the development of new infrastructure projects often requires the services of local suppliers, contractors, and service providers. This can lead to increased demand for goods and services, further boosting local businesses and contributing to broader economic growth. Additionally, higher employment levels can lead to increased consumer spending, which supports local markets and stimulates further economic activity.

Partnerships between international investors and local stakeholders are crucial for ensuring that foreign investments align with the broader goals of land reform. Effective collaboration between investors, government agencies, and community representatives helps to ensure that investments support sustainable development and address social equity concerns. These partnerships facilitate the development of projects that not only drive economic growth but also contribute to social and environmental sustainability.

For instance, partnerships with local communities can help investors understand and address the specific needs and priorities of those directly affected by land reform. By involving local stakeholders in the planning and implementation of investment projects, investors can ensure that their initiatives are responsive to local conditions and challenges. This collaborative approach helps to build trust and ensure that the benefits of foreign investment are distributed equitably.

Moreover, responsible foreign investment practices are essential for balancing economic growth with social equity. Investors who adhere to ethical standards and engage in community consultations help to ensure that their projects do not exacerbate existing inequalities or contribute to land dispossession. For example, investors who prioritise environmental sustainability and respect for local land rights are more likely to support outcomes that align with the principles of equitable land reform. By integrating social and environmental considerations into their investment strategies, international investors can contribute to more sustainable and inclusive land reform outcomes.

The positive impact of foreign investment on land reform is also evident in the development of new business models and value chains. For instance, foreign investors may introduce innovative business models that enhance the efficiency and profitability of agricultural production. These models can include contract farming arrangements, agro-processing ventures, and value-added product development, all of which contribute to the growth and diversification of the agricultural sector. By fostering innovation and supporting the development of new business opportunities, foreign investment can drive economic development and support the goals of land reform.

Overall, the positive effects of foreign investment on land reform in South Africa are multifaceted and significant. The injection of resources and expertise, coupled with investments in infrastructure and job creation, supports the broader objectives of land reform by enhancing productivity, improving access to markets, and fostering economic development. Effective partnerships between international investors and local stakeholders are crucial for ensuring that these investments contribute to social equity and sustainable development. When managed responsibly, foreign investment can play a vital role in advancing land reform goals and supporting the overall progress of South Africa's socio-economic landscape.

Impact of International Partnerships on Local Livelihoods

Several case studies illustrate how international collaboration has positively impacted land reform in South Africa, demonstrating the transformative effects of strategic partnerships and targeted support. These examples highlight the role of international organisations in advancing land reform objectives, enhancing livelihoods, and addressing specific land-related challenges within local communities.

One prominent example of international collaboration in land reform is the Land Tenure Security Initiative, which has significantly improved land tenure for historically dispossessed communities. This initiative, supported by organisations such as the United Nations Development Programme (UNDP) and the World Bank, aimed to formalise land ownership and provide legal recognition to communities that lacked secure land tenure.

The initiative began with a comprehensive approach to mapping and documenting land holdings. International experts worked closely with local communities to conduct detailed surveys that captured accurate data on land use patterns and historical claims. This process was essential for establishing a clear and legal framework for land ownership. The next step involved the formalisation of land rights through the issuance of land titles to eligible individuals and groups. This formalisation process provided legal security and reduced the risk of land disputes, which had been a persistent issue for many communities.

The impact of the Land Tenure Security Initiative has been profound and multifaceted. For many community members, receiving formal land titles has empowered them to invest in their properties and undertake long-term development projects. Farmers, for example, gained access to agricultural loans and grants, which enabled them to invest in modern farming techniques and infrastructure. Investments in irrigation systems, improved seed varieties, and advanced farming equipment have led to increased productivity and better crop yields. This, in turn, has enhanced food security and economic stability for local communities.

Additionally, the provision of secure land tenure has fostered greater social cohesion within these communities. By addressing uncertainties and conflicts related to land ownership, the initiative has contributed to a more stable social environment. Community members have been able to engage more actively in local development activities and governance processes, fostering a sense of ownership and collective responsibility. This strengthened social fabric has further supported the success of land reform efforts, as communities are better equipped to manage and sustain the benefits of formalised land rights.

Another successful case study of international collaboration involves community development projects focused on addressing specific land-related challenges. Organisations such as Oxfam and ActionAid have played pivotal roles in implementing these projects, which target key areas such as agricultural practices and land management.

One illustrative example is a project aimed at improving agricultural productivity among smallholder farmers in rural South Africa. This project, supported by international funding and technical expertise, sought to enhance farming practices and support sustainable land management. International organisations collaborated with local communities to identify their needs and develop tailored solutions that addressed specific challenges.

The project included a variety of components designed to improve agricultural practices. Farmers received training in modern techniques such as conservation tillage, which helps maintain soil health and reduce erosion. The project also introduced organic farming practices, which promote soil fertility and reduce reliance on chemical inputs. Additionally, integrated pest management techniques were implemented to control pests more effectively while minimising environmental impact.

Infrastructure development was another key component of the project. Investments were made in irrigation systems, which provided reliable water sources for crops and reduced dependence on erratic rainfall. The project also supported the construction of storage facilities, which enabled farmers to store their produce safely and sell it when market conditions were more favourable. Improved access to market roads facilitated the transportation of agricultural products to local and regional markets, allowing farmers to reach buyers more efficiently and secure better prices.

The success of this community development project is evident in the tangible improvements experienced by local farmers. Reports from participants indicate significant increases in crop yields, higher income levels, and enhanced soil health. For example, farmers in project areas reported substantial gains in their agricultural output, allowing them to diversify their crops and increase their food security. The infrastructure investments also contributed to the efficiency of agricultural operations, reducing post-harvest losses and improving overall market access.

A further example of successful International collaboration is the integrated land and water management initiatives that have been implemented in various parts of South Africa. These initiatives have involved partnerships between international organisations, local governments, and community stakeholders to address challenges related to land degradation, water scarcity, and sustainable resource management.

One such initiative focused on improving land and water management practices in a semi-arid region of South Africa. The project aimed to combat land degradation and enhance water conservation through a combination of technical support, community engagement, and infrastructure development. International organisations provided expertise in areas such as soil conservation, water harvesting, and sustainable land use planning.

The project included the implementation of soil conservation measures, such as terracing and contour ploughing, to reduce erosion and improve soil fertility. Water harvesting techniques, such as the construction of check dams and rainwater collection systems, were introduced to capture and store water for agricultural use. Additionally, the project supported the development of community-based water management committees, which were responsible for overseeing the sustainable use and maintenance of water resources.

The outcomes of this Integrated land and water management initiative have been highly positive. The implementation of soil conservation measures and water harvesting techniques has led to improvements in soil health, increased agricultural productivity, and better water availability for farming. The establishment of community-based water management committees has empowered local communities to take an active role in managing their resources, leading to more sustainable and equitable outcomes.

Economic Development through International Collaboration in Land Reform

In addition to specific projects, international collaboration has also supported broader efforts to integrate land reform with economic development. One notable case study involves a partnership between international donors, South African government agencies, and private sector actors to promote land reform through economic development initiatives.

This collaboration focused on creating economic opportunities for land reform beneficiaries by supporting the development of small and medium-sized enterprises (SMMEs) and promoting local entrepreneurship. International organisations provided funding, technical assistance, and capacity-building support to help new landowners establish and grow their businesses. This support included business training, access to finance, and mentorship programmes.

The initiative also aimed to link land reform beneficiaries with existing value chains and market opportunities. For example, new landowners were connected with established agribusinesses and cooperatives, enabling them to participate in larger supply chains and access new markets. This approach helped to integrate land reform beneficiaries into the broader economy and create sustainable livelihoods.

The impact of this economic development-focused approach to land reform has been significant. Many beneficiaries have successfully established and expanded their businesses, contributing to local economic growth and job creation. The integration of land reform with economic development has also helped to build resilience and sustainability into the land reform process, ensuring that the benefits of land ownership are maximised and sustained over the long term.

These case studies illustrate the diverse and positive impacts of international collaboration on land reform in South Africa. The successful implementation of land tenure security initiatives, community development projects, integrated land and water management efforts, and economic development programmes demonstrates how strategic partnerships and targeted support can drive meaningful improvements in land reform outcomes. By leveraging international expertise, resources, and funding, South Africa has been able to advance its land reform agenda and enhance the livelihoods of historically disadvantaged communities.

The lessons learned from these case studies underscore the importance of continued international support and collaboration in achieving land reform goals. Effective partnerships between international organisations, local communities, and government agencies are essential for addressing ongoing challenges and ensuring that land reform initiatives are successful and sustainable. By building on the successes of past projects and exploring new opportunities for collaboration, South Africa can continue to make progress towards a more equitable and inclusive land reform process.

International influence has played a profoundly positive role in the slow progress of South Africa's land reform journey. The global emphasis on human rights, combined with the support of foreign aid and investment, has significantly advanced the country's efforts to address land injustices. By embracing the positive aspects of international involvement and strategically engaging with global actors, South Africa can continue to advance its land reform goals and work towards a more equitable and just land distribution system. The collaboration between local and international stakeholders underscores the importance of global support in achieving social justice and equity in land distribution.

Conclusion

Debunking the belief held by some South Africans of European descent that land expropriation without compensation could deter potential investors and harm the country's economic prospects is essential. This notion oversimplifies and misrepresents the broader realities of land reform and investment dynamics. The assertion that expropriation will necessarily lead to a decline in investment overlooks several crucial factors.

Firstly, investors are often more concerned with the stability and transparency of land governance than with the specifics of land ownership. Effective land reform, when conducted transparently and with clear legal frameworks, can actually enhance investment prospects by providing more secure and equitable land tenure systems. Such systems reduce conflicts and uncertainties over land use, which are attractive features for potential investors.

Secondly, many countries with successful land reform programmes have demonstrated that it is possible to attract significant foreign investment even with robust land reform policies. These countries have shown that investment does not automatically diminish in the face of equitable land distribution; rather, it often thrives in an environment where land rights are clearly defined and protected. For instance, countries like Rwanda and Bolivia have managed to attract international investment while implementing substantial land reforms, highlighting that equitable land distribution can coexist with a healthy investment climate.

Thirdly, the fear that land expropriation will scare off investors assumes that all investment is solely motivated by the availability of cheap land. In reality, investors consider a range of factors, including market potential, economic stability, and regulatory environment. By addressing historical injustices and creating a more inclusive land ownership system, South Africa could actually improve its attractiveness to ethical investors who value social responsibility and long-term stability over short-term gains.

Furthermore, the South African government's approach to land reform has consistently included provisions to protect existing investments and ensure fair compensation where necessary. This approach mitigates the risk of creating an investment-hostile environment. The government's commitment to balancing land reform with investor protection helps maintain confidence in the country's economic stability and regulatory environment.

Additionally, evidence suggests that the impact of land reform on investment is not uniformly negative. For instance, in countries that have successfully implemented land reform, there has been a positive correlation between improved land rights and increased agricultural productivity. This increase in productivity often attracts investment in the agribusiness sector, as investors seek to capitalise on enhanced agricultural output and more predictable land use conditions. This correlation indicates that land reform can create a more favourable investment climate by enhancing land productivity and providing investors with more secure and stable conditions.

Moreover, the argument that land expropriation will deter investors fails to acknowledge the potential for new, innovative investment opportunities that land reform might unlock. As land ownership becomes more equitable, there could be new opportunities for small and medium-sized enterprises (SMMEs) and community-based businesses, which can drive local economic development and create a more diverse and resilient economy. By supporting the growth of SMMEs, land reform can stimulate local entrepreneurship and contribute to broader economic growth.

Finally, it is essential to recognise that the successful implementation of land reform is contingent upon careful planning, clear legal frameworks, and effective management. When these elements are in place, land reform can coexist with a thriving investment environment. Effective land reform can align with broader economic goals and attract investment by fostering a more stable and just economic environment. Thus, rather than deterring investment, a well-managed land expropriation process can complement economic growth and attract investment by creating a more predictable and equitable land tenure system.

In summary, international perspectives, foreign aid, global organisations, and foreign investment have collectively shaped South Africa's land reform efforts. These external forces have driven the progress of land reform initiatives, contributing to the country's pursuit of a more equitable and just land distribution system. The influence of these international factors underscores the interconnected nature of global and local efforts in addressing land reform challenges. As South

Africa continues to navigate its land reform journey, the impact of these international influences will remain significant.

The ongoing engagement with global perspectives, the continued support of foreign aid, the collaboration with global and regional organisations, and the management of foreign investment will all play critical roles in shaping the future of land reform in South Africa. Balancing these influences with domestic priorities and ensuring that land reform efforts achieve their intended outcomes will be essential for the success of South Africa's land reform agenda.

10. THE PATH FORWARD: SHAPING THE FUTURE OF LAND REFORM IN SOUTH AFRICA

As South Africa stands at a critical juncture in its land reform journey, it is essential to take a moment to reflect on the progress made thus far and to envision the path forward with renewed clarity and determination. The country has navigated a complex and often contentious landscape of land reform, marked by both successes and setbacks. At this pivotal moment, it is crucial to synthesise the key insights gleaned from previous discussions, thoroughly examine the remaining challenges, and propose innovative strategies that can propel the land reform agenda towards its ultimate goal of achieving a more equitable and just land distribution system.

Over the years, South Africa has made significant strides in addressing the historical injustices of land dispossession. The progress achieved has been the result of tireless efforts by government institutions, civil society organisations, and the communities most affected by these issues. These efforts have provided valuable lessons that must now be leveraged to guide the next phase of land reform. By critically evaluating the successes and shortcomings of past initiatives, the country can better understand what has worked, what has not, and why. This reflection is not merely an academic exercise but a necessary step in ensuring that the future of land reform is informed by practical experience and grounded in reality.

One of the key insights from the land reform journey so far is the importance of inclusivity and community engagement. Successful land reform initiatives have often been those that have actively involved the voices of the people on the ground—those who have the most at stake in the outcomes of these policies. Their experiences, struggles, and aspirations must continue to shape the direction of land reform, ensuring that the policies implemented are not only technically sound but also socially just. This approach requires a commitment to participatory processes, where affected communities are not merely consulted but are central to decision-making.

However, significant challenges remain. The pace of land reform has been slower than many had hoped, hampered by a range of factors including bureaucratic inefficiencies, legal complexities, and political constraints. Moreover, the question of how to balance the need for land redistribution with the protection of property rights and the promotion of economic stability continues to be a source of tension. Addressing these challenges will require innovative thinking and a willingness to explore new approaches that go beyond the conventional paradigms of land reform.

One such approach is the integration of technology and data-driven solutions in the land reform process. Advances in geospatial technology, for example, can enhance the accuracy and efficiency of land surveys, making it easier to identify and allocate land for redistribution. Additionally, the use of digital platforms can improve transparency and accountability in the administration of land reform, ensuring that resources are allocated fairly and that the process is accessible to all stakeholders.

Another innovative strategy involves strengthening partnerships between the public and private sectors. While land reform is primarily a government-led initiative, the private sector can play a crucial role in supporting these efforts through investment, expertise, and resources. By fostering collaboration between these sectors, South Africa can create a more dynamic and sustainable land reform process that benefits from the strengths of both public institutions and private enterprises.

As South Africa moves forward, it is also essential to consider the role of international cooperation in advancing land reform. The global community has been a significant player in shaping South Africa's land reform policies, providing both financial assistance and policy guidance. Continued engagement with international partners can offer valuable insights and support, particularly in areas such as capacity building, technical assistance, and the sharing of best practices.

South Africa's land reform journey is at a crossroads. The progress made thus far provides a solid foundation, but there is still much work to be done. By reflecting on past experiences, addressing ongoing challenges, and embracing innovative strategies, South Africa can continue to advance towards a more equitable and just land distribution system. This final chapter is not an end but a new beginning—an opportunity to chart a course that not only rectifies the injustices of the past but also lays the groundwork for a future where land reform is a catalyst for social justice, economic empowerment, and national unity.

Throughout this book, we have embarked on an in-depth exploration of the multifaceted nature of land reform in South Africa, tracing its deep historical roots, examining the evolution of policy frameworks, and considering the considerable influence of international dynamics. This journey has provided a comprehensive view of the progress made in addressing the profound historical injustices associated with land dispossession and in promoting a more equitable distribution of land. The advancements achieved thus far are a testament to the resilience and determination of individuals, communities, and institutions committed to transforming South Africa's socio-political and economic landscape.

The history of land In South Africa is one marked by deep-seated inequities, rooted in centuries of colonial and apartheid-era policies that systematically dispossessed the majority of the population of their land. The journey of land reform, as we have examined, has been one of attempting to right these historical wrongs, aiming to restore land to those who were unjustly deprived of it and to create a more just and equitable society. The policies that have been developed over the years reflect a complex interplay of legal, economic, and social considerations, each designed to address the myriad challenges associated with such an ambitious undertaking.

Significant progress has been made in this regard, and the successes achieved thus far should not be underestimated. Through various legislative and policy measures, many South Africans have gained access to land that was previously beyond their reach, and there has been a concerted effort to ensure that this land is used productively and sustainably. These achievements have been driven by the hard work and dedication of those on the ground—community leaders, activists, and government officials—who have tirelessly advocated for a more equitable land distribution system.

However, as this book has also revealed, the journey towards comprehensive land reform is far from complete. Persistent challenges continue to hinder the full realisation of a just and inclusive land tenure system. Bureaucratic inefficiencies, legal complexities, and socio-political tensions remain significant obstacles that must be navigated. These issues are not merely technical in nature; they are deeply intertwined with the broader socio-economic realities of South Africa, where disparities in wealth, power, and access to resources continue to influence the pace and direction of land reform.

One of the most critical challenges is the slow pace of land redistribution, which has often fallen short of expectations. Despite the best efforts of those involved, the process of identifying, acquiring, and redistributing land has been fraught with delays and difficulties. These challenges have been exacerbated by conflicting interests and priorities among various stakeholders, including landowners, government bodies, and communities. Additionally, there is the ongoing challenge of ensuring that land reform does not merely transfer ownership but also empowers new landowners to use their land effectively and sustainably, thus contributing to broader economic development and food security.

The role of international influences, as we have discussed, adds another layer of complexity to the land reform process. Global perspectives, foreign aid, and the involvement of international organisations have played a significant role in shaping South Africa's land reform policies. While these influences have provided valuable support and guidance, they have also introduced additional considerations that must be balanced with domestic priorities. The interplay between global and local factors highlights the interconnectedness of South Africa's land reform efforts with broader international trends in human rights, economic development, and social justice.

The examination of these themes throughout the book underscores the inherent complexity of land reform, a process that intertwines legal, social, economic, and political threads. Achieving a just and inclusive land tenure system is not a simple task; it requires continued commitment, innovative thinking, and adaptive strategies that respond to the evolving challenges and opportunities of the present moment. The insights gained from this exploration serve as a call to action for all stakeholders involved in land reform—from policymakers and legal experts to community leaders and international partners—to persist in their efforts and to work collaboratively towards common goals.

In reflecting on the progress made and the challenges that remain, it is clear that land reform in South Africa is not just about redistributing land; it is about transforming society. It is about addressing the deep-seated inequalities that have long plagued the country and creating a foundation for a more just and equitable future. The work of land reform is, therefore, not just a policy objective but a moral imperative, one that demands ongoing attention, dedication, and innovation.

As South Africa moves forward, the lessons learned from past experiences must guide the path ahead. The challenges that remain are daunting, but they are not insurmountable. With careful planning, clear legal frameworks, and effective management, land reform can achieve its goals and contribute to the broader objectives of economic growth, social justice, and national unity. The success of land reform will depend on the ability of all stakeholders to work together, to build on the progress made, and to address the challenges that lie ahead with creativity and resolve.

This book has sought to provide a comprehensive understanding of the complexities of land reform in South Africa. The journey has been long and challenging, but it has also been marked by significant achievements. As the country continues to navigate this complex and often contentious issue, it is crucial to remember that the ultimate goal of land reform is to create a more just, equitable, and inclusive society. The road ahead may be difficult, but with continued effort and collaboration, South Africa can achieve this vision and secure a better future for all its people.

Addressing Persistent Challenges in Land Reform

Despite the significant strides made in land reform, several critical challenges persist that must be addressed to ensure the ongoing success of the reform process. One of the primary issues is the uneven distribution of land. Although progress has been achieved in redistributing land, disparities remain, with certain areas receiving more attention and resources than others. This uneven distribution undermines the goal of achieving equitable land access and perpetuates existing inequalities, leaving some communities with insufficient or no access to land while others benefit disproportionately.

Another major challenge is the inefficiency within legal and administrative processes related to land reform. The bureaucratic hurdles and complex legal frameworks can significantly slow down the implementation of land reforms, leading to delays and frustrations for those seeking to benefit from these policies. Administrative inefficiencies further complicate the management of land transactions, often resulting in prolonged disputes and uncertainty for both landowners and beneficiaries. These delays not only affect the individuals involved but also impact the overall effectiveness of the land reform process.

Socio-economic disparities within affected communities also pose significant obstacles. Many communities continue to face poverty and lack access to essential resources needed to make effective use of redistributed land. Without targeted support to address these socio-economic challenges, land reform efforts may fall short of their intended outcomes. The inability to utilise land productively undermines the potential for land reform to create lasting improvements in the livelihoods of those most in need, failing to address the root causes of inequality and poverty.

To address these challenges effectively, a comprehensive approach is required. This involves re-evaluating and refining land reform policies to better address existing gaps and ensure they are responsive to the needs of all stakeholders. Policy adjustments should focus on enhancing fairness in land distribution and incorporating feedback from affected communities to improve policy effectiveness and inclusivity.

Improved land administration practices are also crucial. Streamlining and modernising land administration processes can reduce inefficiencies and expedite the resolution of land disputes. Implementing technology-driven solutions can enhance transparency and accuracy in land management, making it easier to track land ownership and transactions. By leveraging technology, the management of land records and transactions can become more efficient, reducing delays and improving overall effectiveness.

Providing targeted support for disadvantaged groups is essential to enable beneficiaries to make productive use of their land. This support might include access to financial resources, training, and technical assistance, which are crucial for fostering economic development and reducing socio-economic disparities. Without such support, the potential benefits of land reform may not be fully realised, and the intended improvements in livelihoods may not materialise.

Resolving land disputes swiftly and fairly is another critical element. Developing mechanisms for effective dispute resolution can prevent conflicts from hindering the progress of land reform. This may involve establishing dedicated bodies or improving existing processes to handle land-related conflicts, ensuring that disputes are resolved in a manner that is fair and efficient.

Enhancing the capacity of institutions responsible for land management is also vital. Strengthening these institutions involves investing in staff training, improving coordination between agencies, and ensuring that institutions are adequately equipped to fulfil their roles. By building institutional capacity, the administration and management of land reform processes can be improved, leading to more effective implementation and oversight.

By addressing these issues through a comprehensive and coordinated approach, South Africa can improve the effectiveness of its land reform policies and contribute to a more equitable and just land tenure system. Continued commitment to these efforts will be essential for achieving the long-term goals of land reform, ensuring that its benefits are widely and fairly distributed, and making meaningful progress towards a more inclusive and equitable society.

To advance land reform efforts, it is crucial to explore and implement innovative strategies that can address existing challenges and enhance the overall effectiveness of the reform process. Embracing new policy measures, integrating advanced technological solutions, and adopting participatory community engagement practices are key to driving meaningful progress in this area.

One significant avenue for innovation is the integration of digital technologies into land administration systems. Digital solutions offer the potential to revolutionise how land is managed and recorded. For instance, blockchain technology can be leveraged to create secure and transparent land registries. Blockchain's inherent characteristics, such as its immutability and decentralised nature, ensure that land ownership records are secure and resistant to tampering or fraud. This can greatly enhance the reliability of land transactions, providing a robust system for tracking and verifying ownership.

Additionally, Geographic Information Systems (GIS) represent another technological advancement with considerable potential for improving land administration. GIS technology facilitates the precise mapping of land parcels and allows for the detailed monitoring of land use changes over time. By providing accurate and up-to-date information, GIS can aid in better land management and planning, ensuring that land reform policies are implemented effectively and that land resources are utilised in a sustainable manner. The ability to visualise and analyse spatial data can also support more informed decision-making processes, helping to identify areas that require targeted intervention or support.

Integrating these digital technologies into land administration can streamline administrative processes, reduce bureaucratic delays, and enhance overall efficiency. By modernising how land is recorded and managed, these technologies can address some of the inefficiencies that have historically plagued traditional land management systems. This can result in faster and more transparent land transactions, ultimately benefiting all stakeholders involved in the land reform process.

In addition to technological advancements, enhancing community engagement through participatory approaches is vital for the success of land reform initiatives. Involving communities in decision-making processes ensures that their needs and concerns are directly addressed. When communities are actively engaged in discussions about how land is redistributed and managed, the reforms are more likely to be relevant and effective. This participatory approach fosters a sense of ownership and commitment among community members, as they have a stake in the outcomes of the reform process.

Effective community engagement can be achieved through various methods, such as public consultations, community forums, and collaborative planning sessions. These platforms allow for open dialogue between policymakers and community members, ensuring that the voices of those directly affected by land reform are heard. By incorporating community feedback into policy design and implementation, land reform efforts can be more responsive to local contexts and better aligned with the needs of those most impacted.

By leveraging these innovative strategies, South Africa can address some of the persistent challenges faced by land reform initiatives. The combination of advanced technologies and participatory practices can help overcome issues such as administrative inefficiencies, uneven land distribution, and socio-economic disparities. Embracing innovation in land reform is not just about adopting new tools; it is about creating a more effective and equitable system that can adapt to changing needs and circumstances.

Advancing land reform through innovation requires a commitment to continuously improving and adapting strategies. By integrating digital solutions, enhancing community engagement, and remaining open to new developments, South Africa can make significant strides toward achieving a more just and inclusive land tenure system. This approach will not only address existing gaps but also build a foundation for sustainable and equitable land management in the future.

Robust governance and institutional frameworks are fundamental to the success of land reform efforts. For land reform to be effective, it is crucial that systems managing land distribution, dispute resolution, and policy implementation are transparent and accountable. The success of these processes hinges on the strength of the governance structures that support them.

Strengthening governance frameworks begins with enhancing the capacity of government institutions responsible for land reform. This involves investing in the resources and training necessary to ensure that these institutions can perform their roles effectively. Well-equipped institutions are better able to handle the complexities of land reform, from administering land allocations to resolving disputes. This capacity building also includes improving the skills of staff and updating technological tools to manage land records and transactions more efficiently.

Promoting collaboration among stakeholders is another key aspect of strengthening governance frameworks. Land reform often involves a diverse range of actors, including government agencies, local communities, private sector players, and non-governmental organisations. Effective land reform requires that these stakeholders work together harmoniously, sharing information and coordinating efforts to achieve common goals. Creating platforms for dialogue and collaboration can help align interests, address conflicts, and foster a collective approach to land management.

Ensuring that land reform policies are applied consistently is also crucial. This consistency helps to build trust in the reform process and ensures that all stakeholders are treated fairly. Clear guidelines and standardised procedures should be established to govern land distribution and management. These guidelines should be communicated effectively to all parties involved to prevent misunderstandings and ensure that everyone is aware of their rights and responsibilities.

Effective management practices and oversight mechanisms are essential for maintaining public trust and ensuring that land reform outcomes are realised. Oversight bodies or mechanisms should be established to monitor the implementation of land reform policies and to address any issues that arise. These mechanisms need to be independent and well-resourced to carry out their functions effectively.

Regular audits, evaluations, and public reports can help ensure transparency and accountability, demonstrating that land reform processes are being conducted fairly and that resources are being used efficiently.

Overall, robust governance and institutional frameworks are critical to the success of land reform. By enhancing the capacity of government institutions, fostering stakeholder collaboration, and ensuring consistent policy application, South Africa can create a solid foundation for effective land reform. This, in turn, will help to maintain public trust and achieve the desired outcomes of land reform, contributing to a more equitable and just land distribution system.

Unlocking Economic Potential Through Land Reform: A Path to Sustainable Growth

Land reform presents significant opportunities for economic development, and aligning it with broader economic goals can drive growth and create sustainable livelihoods. To fully harness these opportunities, it is essential to integrate land reform initiatives with strategies that promote economic development and enhance productivity.

Supporting the development of small and medium-sized enterprises (SMMEs) is a crucial aspect of this integration. SMMEs play a vital role in local economies by generating employment, fostering innovation, and contributing to economic diversification. By providing land to support the establishment and expansion of SMMEs, land reform can stimulate entrepreneurial activity and create new economic opportunities. This support can include access to affordable land, financial resources, and business development services, which are essential for enabling new enterprises to thrive.

Fostering local entrepreneurship is another important strategy. Encouraging entrepreneurial initiatives within communities can help drive economic growth and improve livelihoods. Land reform can facilitate this by ensuring that land is accessible for business ventures and by offering incentives or support for local entrepreneurs. Training and mentorship programmes can further empower individuals to start and manage their own businesses, leading to increased economic activity and resilience.

Investment in infrastructure is also vital for enhancing the economic impact of land reform. Developing infrastructure such as irrigation systems can significantly improve agricultural productivity. Reliable irrigation is crucial for increasing crop yields and ensuring sustainable agricultural practices, which in turn can support local food security and economic stability. Additionally, improving market access through better transport and logistics infrastructure can enable farmers and businesses to reach broader markets, boosting their revenue and economic viability.

Integrating land reform with broader economic development strategies also involves creating an environment that supports growth and investment. This can include streamlining regulatory processes, offering tax incentives, and fostering a supportive business climate. By addressing barriers to investment and creating a favourable environment for economic activity, land reform can contribute to a more dynamic and competitive economic landscape.

Overall, by aligning land reform with economic development goals, South Africa can create a synergy that drives growth and improves the overall economic landscape. The integration of land reform with strategies that support SMMEs, local entrepreneurship, and infrastructure development can stimulate economic activity, enhance productivity, and foster sustainable livelihoods. This comprehensive approach ensures that land reform not only addresses historical injustices but also contributes to long-term economic prosperity and stability.

Ensuring that land reform policies are inclusive and socially just is crucial for achieving equitable outcomes and building a fair land tenure system. To realise these goals, it is essential to actively engage affected communities throughout the reform process. This engagement helps ensure that the policies address the specific needs and concerns of those most impacted by land reform.

One fundamental strategy for fostering inclusivity is the implementation of targeted support programmes. These programmes can provide assistance tailored to the unique needs of different groups, such as smallholder farmers, disadvantaged communities, and low-income families. By offering targeted support, such as financial assistance, technical training, and resources for land development, land reform can more effectively meet the needs of various stakeholders and promote equitable land distribution.

Promoting gender equity in land ownership is another key aspect of ensuring social justice in land reform. Historically, women have often been disadvantaged in land ownership and access. To address this imbalance, policies should include measures that support women's land rights, such as legal reforms to recognise and protect women's ownership and inheritance rights. Providing women with equal opportunities to acquire and manage land is essential for achieving gender equality and empowering women economically and socially.

Addressing the needs of marginalised groups is also vital for a just land reform process. Marginalised communities, including indigenous peoples, people with disabilities, and other disadvantaged groups, often face unique challenges in accessing land and resources. Land reform policies should incorporate measures to specifically support these groups, ensuring that their rights are recognised and their needs are met. This might include establishing legal protections, providing additional resources, and ensuring that their voices are heard in decision-making processes.

By prioritising social justice and inclusivity, South Africa can build a more equitable land tenure system that enhances social cohesion and fosters a sense of fairness among all stakeholders. Engaging communities, promoting gender equity, and addressing the needs of marginalised groups are essential steps toward ensuring that the benefits of land reform are distributed fairly and that the reform process contributes to a more just and harmonious society. This approach not only addresses historical inequalities but also strengthens the social fabric by creating a more inclusive and equitable land management system.

South Africa stands to gain significantly from examining international experiences in land reform. Successful case studies from other countries offer valuable insights into effective strategies and practices that have proven successful elsewhere. By analysing these experiences, South Africa can identify best practices that might be adapted to its own context, thereby enhancing the effectiveness of its land reform efforts and avoiding common pitfalls encountered in other settings.

International case studies can provide practical examples of how different approaches to land reform have worked in various environments. These examples can reveal innovative solutions, successful policy frameworks, and effective implementation techniques. Learning from these experiences can help South Africa design and implement strategies that are more likely to achieve its land reform goals while avoiding mistakes made by others. For instance, lessons learned from countries that have successfully integrated technology into land administration, managed large-scale land redistribution, or effectively resolved land disputes can be particularly valuable.

Furthermore, continued international collaboration and support are essential for advancing land reform in South Africa. Engaging with global perspectives allows for the incorporation of diverse viewpoints and expertise, which can enrich the reform process. International organisations, development agencies, and foreign governments can offer technical assistance, funding, and guidance, all of which are critical for supporting comprehensive and effective land reform initiatives.

Leveraging international expertise can also provide South Africa with access to cutting-edge research, best practices, and proven methodologies. By participating in global networks and forums dedicated to land reform, South Africa can stay informed about the latest developments and innovations in the field. This engagement can help ensure that land reform efforts are aligned with global standards and trends, making them more robust and effective.

Learning from international experiences and fostering global collaboration are crucial for enhancing land reform efforts in South Africa. By adopting best practices from successful case studies, avoiding common pitfalls, and engaging with international expertise, South Africa can improve the design and implementation of its land reform policies. This approach not only enhances the effectiveness of land reform but also contributes to achieving long-term goals of equity and sustainable development.

Looking ahead, the vision for land reform in South Africa should centre on establishing a more equitable and just land distribution system. This vision encompasses several critical goals, including achieving widespread land tenure security, promoting sustainable land use practices, and fostering economic development through land reform.

Achieving widespread land tenure security is fundamental to this vision. Ensuring that all landholders have clear and legally recognised rights to their land provides stability and confidence, which is essential for productive land use and investment. Secure land tenure protects individuals and communities from displacement and encourages long-term planning and development.

Promoting sustainable land use practices is another key component of the vision. Sustainable land management not only helps to preserve natural resources and maintain environmental health but also supports the long-term viability of agricultural and economic activities. By encouraging practices that balance productivity with environmental stewardship, South Africa can enhance food security, protect ecosystems, and support resilient communities.

Fostering economic development through land reform involves leveraging land as a catalyst for growth and opportunity. This includes supporting smallholder farmers, encouraging local entrepreneurship, and investing in infrastructure that enhances market access and productivity. By integrating land reform with broader economic strategies, South Africa can create new economic opportunities, generate employment, and stimulate overall economic growth.

The future of land reform will depend on the commitment and collaboration of all stakeholders, including government, civil society, and the private sector. Government agencies must lead with strong policy frameworks, effective implementation strategies, and transparent governance. Civil society organisations can advocate for the needs of affected communities, ensure that voices are heard, and hold institutions accountable. The private sector can contribute through investment, innovation, and partnerships that support land reform goals.

By working together and staying focused on the principles of justice and equity, South Africa can realise its vision of a fair and inclusive land tenure system. This collective effort will help address historical injustices, promote social cohesion, and build a foundation for sustainable development. With a shared commitment to these principles, South Africa can create a land reform process that not only addresses past inequities but also paves the way for a more just and prosperous future.

As we conclude this comprehensive exploration of South Africa's land reform journey, it is crucial to issue a powerful call to action for policymakers, stakeholders, and citizens. The continued advancement of the land reform agenda relies on sustained engagement, collaboration, and commitment from all sectors of society.

Policymakers have a pivotal role in driving land reform forward. Their responsibilities include not only the effective design and implementation of land reform policies but also the rigorous monitoring of progress and adaptation to emerging challenges. Effective implementation involves translating policy into practice, ensuring that reforms are executed efficiently and fairly.

Policymakers must establish mechanisms to track progress, evaluate outcomes, and identify areas for improvement. This involves setting up feedback loops, conducting regular reviews, and making data-driven adjustments to policies as needed. Addressing emerging challenges requires foresight and flexibility, as land reform is an evolving process influenced by social, economic, and environmental factors. Policymakers must be proactive in identifying potential issues and adapting strategies to ensure that reforms remain relevant and effective.

Stakeholders, including civil society organisations, private sector players, and local leaders, must also play an active role in the land reform process. Civil society organisations can provide crucial insights and advocacy, representing the interests of communities and ensuring that reforms address real needs. They can facilitate dialogue, support grassroots mobilisation, and advocate for equitable policy outcomes.

The private sector, through investment and innovation, can contribute to the successful implementation of land reform by supporting agricultural development, infrastructure projects, and entrepreneurial initiatives. Local leaders and community organisations are instrumental in bridging the gap between policy and practice, ensuring that land reform initiatives are grounded In local realities and addressing specific community needs. Their involvement helps ensure that policies are not only theoretically sound but also practically effective and responsive to those directly impacted.

Citizens have a critical role in supporting and advancing land reform efforts. Engaging in community activities, advocating for individual and collective rights, and participating in decision-making processes are essential for driving reform forward. Active civic participation helps ensure that land reform policies are grounded in the needs and aspirations of the people they affect. By voicing their concerns, providing feedback, and actively participating in local and national forums, citizens can help shape the direction of land reform and hold policymakers accountable. This involvement fosters transparency, builds public trust, and ensures that the voices of those directly impacted by land reform are heard and considered.

Conclusion

In summary, the future of land reform in South Africa is intricately linked to the lessons learned from past experiences and the innovative approaches that can be adopted moving forward. To achieve a fair and equitable land tenure system, it is essential to address existing challenges, seize new opportunities, and promote inclusivity. The commitment and collaboration of all stakeholders are crucial to realising this vision. By maintaining a focus on the principles of justice and equity, South Africa can continue to make significant progress in land reform, creating a more just and inclusive land distribution system that supports sustainable development and social cohesion.

The path forward requires a collective effort, with each group playing a specific and vital role. Policymakers must lead with determination and adaptability, stakeholders must contribute their expertise and advocacy, and citizens must engage actively and constructively. Together, these efforts will help ensure that land reform is not just a policy initiative but a transformative process that enhances fairness, equity, and prosperity for all South Africans.

CONCLUSION: UNITY AND JUSTICE THROUGH LAND EXPROPRIATION

In *Land of the Ancestors: Expropriation a Necessity for Justice*, we have embarked on a comprehensive exploration of the complex and multifaceted landscape of land reform in South Africa. This journey has taken us deep into the historical injustices that have been inflicted upon our ancestors, revealing the long-lasting impact of these wrongs on current land distribution. We have also examined the current policies and strategies designed to address these injustices and the role of land expropriation without compensation in this process.

Each chapter has illuminated different aspects of land reform, highlighting the critical importance of land expropriation without compensation in achieving true justice and economic equity. Our exploration began with a thorough analysis of the historical context, tracing the origins of land dispossession and its profound effects on indigenous communities. The legacy of these injustices has shaped the current landscape, creating a pressing need for reform.

We have delved into the evolution of land reform policies, evaluating their effectiveness in redressing historical wrongs and their capacity to promote equitable land distribution. Through detailed case studies, we have examined how various policies have been implemented and their outcomes, both positive and negative. These analyses provide a nuanced understanding of the challenges and opportunities associated with land reform.

The book has also explored the theoretical and practical dimensions of land expropriation without compensation. This policy is not just a legal mechanism but a vital component of a broader justice framework. It represents a necessary intervention to correct historical imbalances, return land to those who have been historically disenfranchised, and create new economic opportunities for marginalised communities. By examining international experiences and comparisons, we have identified best practices and potential pitfalls that can inform South Africa's approach to land reform.

Our discussions have highlighted the importance of integrating land reform with principles of fairness, inclusivity, and sustainability. Effective land reform must go beyond mere policy changes; it requires a comprehensive approach that includes legal reforms, community engagement, and support for sustainable development. Ensuring that land reform efforts are inclusive and equitable is crucial for achieving lasting and meaningful outcomes.

As we conclude this exploration, it is evident that advancing land reform in South Africa demands ongoing commitment and collaboration from all sectors of society. Policymakers must prioritise effective implementation, monitor progress rigorously, and address emerging challenges with flexibility and foresight. Stakeholders, including civil society organisations, the private sector, and local leaders, must actively contribute to policy development, advocate for equitable outcomes, and support the practical implementation of reforms. Citizens, too, play a crucial role by engaging in community activities, advocating for their rights, and participating in decision-making processes.

The Insights gained throughout this book underscore the need for a concerted and strategic effort to achieve a just and equitable land distribution system. By staying true to the principles of justice, inclusivity, and sustainability, South Africa can continue to make significant progress in land reform. This progress will honour the legacy of our ancestors and secure a fair and prosperous future for all citizens. The journey towards a more equitable land tenure system is ongoing, and it requires the dedication and collaboration of everyone involved to realise the vision of justice and economic equity.

The historical backdrop of white settler brutality has significantly underscored the urgent need for systemic change in South Africa. This brutal legacy of land dispossession and racial injustice has created deep-seated inequities that persist today, making it clear that a fundamental transformation in land management and distribution is essential for addressing these historical wrongs.

The evolution of land reform policies over the years reveals a troubling pattern of inadequate redress and persistent inequality. Despite various attempts at reform, the current approaches have often fallen short of delivering the comprehensive and equitable outcomes needed. The incremental and sometimes fragmented nature of past policies has failed to fully address the entrenched disparities and systemic issues that continue to affect marginalised communities. This inadequacy highlights the need for more robust, inclusive, and effective strategies that can truly tackle the legacy of historical injustices.

In contrast, the economic benefits of land expropriation without compensation present a compelling case for systemic change. Expropriating land without compensation offers a significant opportunity to rectify historical injustices by redistributing land to those who have been dispossessed and marginalised. This policy not only addresses the historical wrongs but also has the potential to drive substantial economic benefits. By reallocating land to individuals and communities that have been historically disenfranchised, land expropriation can foster economic empowerment, promote entrepreneurial activity, and enhance productivity.

Furthermore, land expropriation without compensation can contribute to sustainable development by enabling more equitable land use and management practices. When land is distributed more fairly, it supports more balanced economic growth and reduces inequalities. This, in turn, creates opportunities for sustainable agricultural practices, improved infrastructure, and enhanced community development.

The historical injustices stemming from white settler brutality have highlighted the pressing need for systemic change in land reform. The evolution of land reform policies has demonstrated the inadequacies of current approaches and the persistent nature of inequality. However, land expropriation without compensation offers a promising path to rectify these historical wrongs and achieve substantial economic and developmental benefits. By embracing more effective and inclusive land reform strategies, South Africa can move towards a more just and equitable land distribution system, addressing past injustices while promoting sustainable development for the future.

The voices from the ground have offered invaluable insights into the lived experiences of those affected by land dispossession, profoundly underscoring the urgent necessity for equitable land distribution. These personal accounts and community perspectives have illuminated the severe impact of historical injustices on individuals and families, highlighting the gaps in current land reform policies. The stories of those directly impacted reveal the tangible consequences of past injustices and reinforce the need for a policy shift that truly aligns with the principles of justice and equality.

The case for regime change in land reform policies has been compelling. Advocates for change argue that the current approach has not adequately addressed the systemic inequalities and injustices that persist. This push for a transformative shift calls for a reimagining of land reform strategies to ensure they are more inclusive, equitable, and responsive to the needs of historically marginalised communities. The call for regime change is not merely about altering policies but about fundamentally transforming the land reform process to address deep-seated issues of inequality and injustice.

In addition to domestic efforts, the positive impact of international influence on land reform cannot be overstated. Global support, coupled with the adoption of best practices from other countries, offers significant opportunities for improving South Africa's land reform framework. International experiences provide valuable lessons in successful policy implementation, innovative land management practices, and effective strategies for addressing historical grievances. By engaging with global perspectives and incorporating proven approaches, South Africa can enhance its land reform policies to better meet the needs of its diverse population.

Looking ahead, the path to meaningful and sustainable change will require a concerted effort from all sectors of society. Policymakers must lead the charge by developing and enacting reforms that are grounded in principles of fairness and equity. This includes designing policies that not only address the historical injustices but also create a framework for ongoing evaluation and adjustment. Effective policy implementation requires robust governance structures, transparent processes, and a commitment to addressing emerging challenges as they arise.

Activists and advocacy groups have a crucial role in this transformative process. Their efforts in raising awareness, mobilizing communities, and advocating for policy changes are essential for driving progress. By pushing for reforms and holding policymakers accountable, these groups ensure that land reform remains a priority and that the voices of those affected are heard and addressed.

Citizens also play an important role in supporting land reform. Engaging in community activities, participating in public discussions, and advocating for equitable policies are ways in which individuals can contribute to the reform process. Citizen involvement helps ensure that land reform initiatives are reflective of and responsive to the needs of the broader community.

The collective efforts of policymakers, activists, and citizens are crucial for championing and implementing the necessary changes for a just and equitable land distribution system. By drawing on international lessons and remaining committed to justice and equality, South Africa can advance its land reform agenda. This will involve addressing historical injustices, promoting sustainable development, and building a fairer future for all. The journey towards a more equitable land tenure system is ongoing, and it will require unwavering dedication and collaborative action from all involved to realise the vision of a just and inclusive society.

Lastly, the journey toward achieving land justice is both a formidable challenge and a promising opportunity. This endeavour necessitates a resolute commitment to addressing the historical injustices that have shaped land distribution in South Africa and to constructing a more equitable and inclusive future. The path to land justice is not just about policy reform but about making a tangible difference in the lives of those who have long been disadvantaged.

The call to action Is clear and urgent: land expropriation without compensation must be embraced as a crucial step towards rectifying historical wrongs and achieving socio-economic transformation. This approach represents more than a policy adjustment; it is an essential measure for addressing deep-seated inequalities and redistributing land in a manner that honours the principles of justice and equity. By supporting this policy, we affirm our commitment to correcting the historical grievances of those who have been systematically dispossessed and marginalised.

Implementing land expropriation without compensation involves navigating a complex landscape of legal, social, and economic considerations. It requires the development of robust legal frameworks, effective administrative practices, and mechanisms for resolving disputes fairly and transparently. Additionally, it is vital to ensure that the benefits of land reform reach those who have been historically disadvantaged, fostering opportunities for economic empowerment and sustainable development.

As we move forward, it is imperative to remain steadfast in our resolve to honour the legacy of our ancestors. This involves acknowledging the sacrifices made by those who fought for justice and ensuring that their struggles lead to meaningful change. By focusing on principles of fairness, inclusivity, and sustainability, we can work towards a land reform process that genuinely serves the interests of all South Africans.

The journey toward land justice also requires active engagement and collaboration from all sectors of society. Policymakers must be proactive in crafting and implementing effective land reform policies, ensuring that they are aligned with the principles of justice and equity. Civil society organisations, activists, and community leaders must continue to advocate for meaningful reforms, raise awareness about the importance of land justice, and mobilise support for equitable policies.

Citizens play a critical role as well. By participating in community discussions, supporting land reform initiatives, and holding policymakers accountable, individuals can contribute to the success of land reform efforts. Engaging in these activities helps ensure that land reform is not only a policy goal but a shared societal commitment to building a more just and equitable land tenure system.

The journey toward land justice is a multifaceted and ongoing process that requires dedication, collaboration, and perseverance. By embracing land expropriation without compensation as a necessary step towards justice and socio-economic transformation, we can make significant strides in addressing historical injustices and promoting a more equitable future. Through collective effort and unwavering commitment, we can honour the legacy of our ancestors and work towards a fair and just land distribution system that benefits all South Africans.

BIBLIOGRAPHY

Andersen L, Granger C, Reis E, Weinhold D, and Wunder S, The Dynamics of Deforestation and Economic Growth in the Brazilian Amazon (Cambridge University Press 2003).

Beck RB, The History of South Africa (Oxford University Press 2011).

Biesele M, Women Like Meat: The Folklore and Foraging Ideology of the Kalahari Ju/'hoan (Indiana University Press 1993).

Cousins B, Land Reform in South Africa: An Overview (PLAAS 2020).

Duff E, Agrarian Reform in Colombia (Praeger 1968).

Economic Freedom Fighters, Land Reform Policy Document (EFF 2013).

Elphick R, Khoikhoi and the Founding of White South Africa (Ravan Press 1985).

Elphick R and Giliomee H (eds), The Shaping of South African Society, 1652-1840 (2nd edn, Wesleyan University Press 1989).

Glen Grey Act 1894 (56 & 57 Vict c 40).

Gordon RJ, 'European Settlements and Indigenous Dispossession in South Africa: A Historical Perspective' (2019).

Greenberg JH, 'Evidence Regarding Bantu Origins' (1972) 13(2) Journal of African Languages and Linguistics.

Group Areas Act 1950, Act 41 of 1950 (South Africa).

Hall RN, Great Zimbabwe, Mashonaland, Rhodesia (Methuen & Co 1905).

Hin LL, Urban Land Reform in China (Palgrave Macmillan 1999).

Human Rights Watch, 'Fast Track Land Reform in Zimbabwe' vol 14, no 1(A) (March 2002) accessed 21 August 2022 https://www.hrw.org/legacy/reports/2002/zimbabwe/index.htm#TopOfPage.

J Malema, 'We are not calling for the slaughter of white people, at least for now' (Speech, EFF Rally, 2016).

Land Restitution Act 1994 (SA).

Lapping B, Apartheid: A History (Macmillan 1986).

Legassick M, The Struggle for the Eastern Cape 1800–1854 (Kegan Paul International 2010).

Lee RB, The !Kung San: A Study in Human Ecology (Cambridge University Press 1979).

Mamdani M, Citizen and Subject: Contemporary Africa and the Legacy of Late Colonialism (Princeton University Press 1996).

Maake S, Land Reform in South Africa: Obstinate Spatial Distortions (Thesis, University of Limpopo).

Maylam P, A History of the African People of South Africa: From the Early Iron Age to the 1970s (David Philip Publishers 1986).

M N Mphahlele, The Indigenous Peoples of South Africa (University of South Africa Press 2011).

Mitchell P, The Archaeology of Southern Africa (Cambridge University Press 2002).

Moseley WG, Land Reform in South Africa (Rowman & Littlefield Publishers 2015).

Mostert N, Frontiers: The Epic of South Africa's Creation and the Tragedy of the Xhosa People (Jonathan Cape 1992).

Ngcukaitobi T, Land Matters: South Africa's Failed Reforms and the Road Ahead (Penguin Random House 2021).

Ngcukaitobi T, The Land Is Ours: South Africa's First Black Lawyers and the Birth of Constitutionalism (Penguin 2018).

Ntsebeza L and Hall R (eds), The Land Question in South Africa: The Challenge of Transformation and Redistribution (HSRC Press 2007).

Parliament of South Africa, 'Constitutional Review Committee: Report on Land Expropriation' (2018).

Peires JB, The House of Phalo: A History of the Xhosa People in the Days of Their Independence (Ravan Press 1981).

Pankhurst D, A Resolvable Conflict? The Politics of Land in Namibia (Ph.D. thesis, University of Bradford 1996).

Posel D, The Making of Apartheid: 1948-1961 (Oxford University Press 1991).

Schapera SR, The Khoisan Peoples of South Africa: Bushmen and Hottentots (Routledge & Kegan Paul 1930).

Seutloali J, 'Speech at The EFF's Regional General Assembly' (2017) [De Aar].

South Africa, Land Reform Act 3 of 1994.

South African Human Rights Commission, 'Land Reform and Human Rights' (2022) https://www.sahrc.org.za/index.php/publications.

The Native Land Act 1913 (SA) s 2.

Thomas E, The Harmless People (Vintage Books 1989).

Thompson L, A History of South Africa (Yale University Press 2001).

Truth and Reconciliation Commission of South Africa, Report (1998).

Vaughan M, Curing Their Ills: Colonial Power and African Illness (Stanford University Press 1991).

Wilmsen E, Land Filled with Flies: A Political Economy of the Kalahari (University of Chicago Press 1989).

Worden N, The Making of Modern South Africa: Conquest, Apartheid, Democracy (Wiley-Blackwell 2012).

World Bank, Land Reform and Poverty Reduction (World Bank 2003).

ABOUT THE AUTHOR

Justice Seutloali is a dedicated political activist, legal scholar, and emerging author from Petrusville in the Northern Cape Province of South Africa. He brings a wealth of experience and insight into the field of land reform through his extensive involvement in political activism and legal scholarship.

With a career spanning over a decade, Justice Seutloali has been deeply engaged in South African politics since the age of 17. His commitment to social justice and equitable land distribution has been a central theme throughout his activism. Notably, he served as the Regional Secretary of the Economic Freedom Fighters (EFF) in the Pixley Ka Seme region, where he played a significant role in advocating for transformative policies aimed at addressing historical injustices.

His passion for land reform and social equity is evident in his writings and public discourse. *Land of the Ancestors: Expropriation a Necessity for Justice* reflects his dedication to advancing the conversation on land expropriation and its role in achieving justice. Justice Seutloali's analytical approach and personal experiences offer a unique perspective on the complexities of land reform in South Africa.